# Cleopatra

# SUTTON POCKET BIOGRAPHIES

*Series Editor C.S. Nicholls*

Highly readable brief lives of those who have played a significant part in history, and whose contributions still influence contemporary culture.

SUTTON POCKET BIOGRAPHIES

# Cleopatra

E. E. RICE

SUTTON PUBLISHING

*for*

*W.J.K.*

First published in the United Kingdom in 1999 by
Sutton Publishing Limited · Phoenix Mill
Thrupp · Stroud · Gloucestershire · GL5 2BU

Reprinted in 2001

British Library Cataloguing in Publication Data
A catalogue record for this book is available from the British Library

ISBN 0 7509 2057 2

Typeset in 13/18 pt Perpetua.
Typesetting and origination by
Sutton Publishing Limited.
Printed in Great Britain by
J.H. Haynes & Co., Ltd, Sparkford.

# CONTENTS

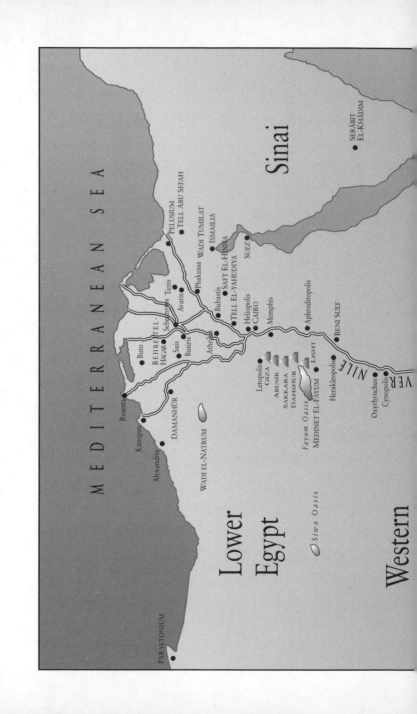

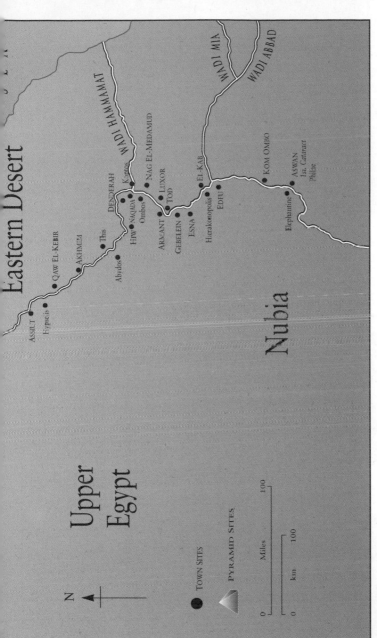

Map of Egypt.

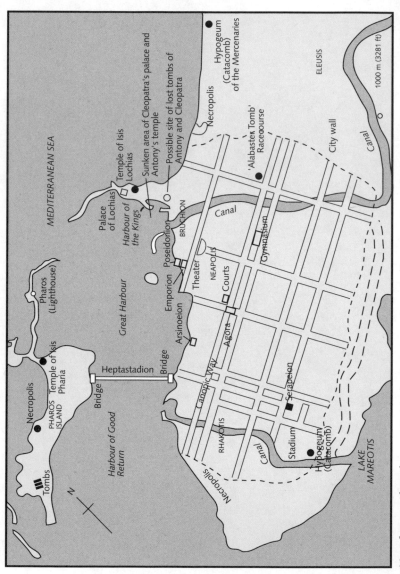

Map of ancient Alexandria.

# CHRONOLOGY

**69 BC**    Birth of Cleopatra (later VII) to Ptolemy XII Auletes and his sister-wife Cleopatra V

**58–55 BC**    Ptolemy Auletes banished from throne of Egypt; rule of his daughters Cleopatra VI (58–57 BC) and Berenike IV (57–55 BC) as pharaohs

**55 BC**    Restoration of Auletes by Aulus Gabinius, Roman governor of Syria

**51 BC**    Death of Auletes; accession of Cleopatra VII to throne of Egypt; marriage to her brother Ptolemy XIII

**49 BC**    Roman civil war between Pompey and Julius Caesar

**48 BC**    Cleopatra driven out of Alexandria by supporters of Ptolemy XIII; assassination of Pompey upon arrival in Egypt; Caesar visits Egypt and meets Cleopatra

**48–47 BC**    'Alexandrian War' fought by Caesar's Roman troops to support Cleopatra against Ptolemy XIII

**47 BC**    Death of Ptolemy XIII after military defeat; Caesar confirms Cleopatra on the throne of Egypt; birth of Caesarion (Ptolemy XV) to Cleopatra and Caesar

**47–44 BC**    Caesar orders Cleopatra to marry and rule jointly with her other brother Ptolemy XIV

# Chronology

| | |
|---|---|
| **46–44 BC** | Cleopatra moves to Rome with Julius Caesar |
| **44 BC** | Assassination of Caesar in Rome on the Ides of March; Cleopatra returns to Alexandria; Ptolemy XIV murdered on Cleopatra's orders |
| **41 BC** | Marc Antony summons Cleopatra to Tarsus |
| **40 BC** | Birth of twins Alexander Helios and Cleopatra Selene to Cleopatra and Antony |
| **37 BC** | Cleopatra 'marries' Antony and he publicly recognizes their children; civil war between Antony and Octavian (later Augustus) threatens |
| **36 BC** | Birth of Ptolemy Philadelphus to Cleopatra and Antony |
| **34 BC** | The so-called 'Donations of Alexandria', when Cleopatra divides her kingdom with her sons |
| **31 BC** | Battle of Actium (September); joint forces of Antony and Cleopatra defeated by Octavian; Antony and Cleopatra escape to Egypt |
| **30 BC** | Suicide of Antony as Octavian enters Alexandria (August), followed by suicide of Cleopatra; Egypt becomes a province of Rome |
| **29 BC** | Octavian celebrates a triumph at Rome for his Egyptian victory |

# INTRODUCTION

Cleopatra VII of Egypt is one of the most famous, if not *the* most famous woman of classical antiquity. Her fortune, or perhaps misfortune, was that the chaotic historical circumstances of the first century BC – namely a series of Roman civil wars combined with the fateful clash of an increasingly powerful Rome with the Hellenistic Empires of the Greek East – brought about her meeting with two of the most famous figures of Roman history, Julius Caesar and Marc Antony. While these encounters dramatically affected the history of the Mediterranean world, it is our own irresistible fascination with love affairs between larger-than-life historical figures that has ensured Cleopatra's undying fame, for better or for worse. Most readers will be familiar with the main events of the story of her relationships with these two men – Caesar's assassination in Rome on the Ides of March in 44 BC, Antony and Cleopatra's defeat by Octavian (later the Roman Emperor Augustus) at the Battle of Actium in 31 BC, and her subsequent suicide allegedly by allowing herself to be bitten by a poisonous asp.

Chapter Two briefly outlines the historical background of the royal Greek Ptolemaic dynasty that ruled Egypt for the last three centuries BC. Suffice it to say here that Cleopatra was the last in the line of Macedonian rulers over a country of immense antiquity, namely the native Egyptian civilization famous today for its pyramids, pharaohs such as Tutankhamun, mummies, and stunning remains of tombs and temples from the last three millennia BC. This culture is probably better known to most readers than the later Ptolemaic Period because of the prevalence of ancient Egyptian artefacts in western museums and the increasing popularity of tourism to that country. Our actual sources for a biography of Cleopatra are few. There are no surviving contemporary Graeco-Egyptian historical accounts that record the end of the Ptolemies. Cleopatra herself had no biographer to relate events from her point of view, and she appears to us as an appendage of the famous Romans with whom fate cast her.

Cleopatra is known to us from a few contemporary Roman historical and literary sources and from later Graeco-Roman historical sources. She inspired a combination of fear and loathing in Roman hearts, and, not surprisingly, this hostility comes across clearly. The governing classes of first-century BC Rome faced a wildly uncertain political situation in the seemingly unstoppable process of change from staunch republic to an empire ruled by forceful personalities. Understandably, Cleopatra was viewed with the utmost suspicion as an 'eastern' queen of luxurious and decadent background and lifestyle, who exercised an evil, corrupting influence over Roman men of affairs. The contemporary Roman poet Horace, although one of the most sensitive of all Latin poets, none the less wrote a chilling poem on the fall of Cleopatra, the opening lines of which probably captured the mood of his countrymen:

> Now is the time to drain the flowing bowl, now with unfettered foot to beat the ground with dancing. . . Before this day it had been wrong to bring our Caecuban [wine] forth from ancient bins, while yet a frenzied queen was plotting ruin 'gainst the Capitol

and destruction to the empire, with her polluted crew of creatures foul with lust – a woman mad enough to nurse the wildest hopes, and drunk with Fortune's favours'. (*Odes*, 1.37.1–12)

Poor Cleopatra.

Relevant ancient historical works are Julius Caesar's *Civil Wars* and the *Alexandrian War*, the first his own account of the struggle for power with his great rival Pompey (known as 'the Great'), and the second a description of the war he later waged in Egypt to restore Cleopatra to her throne in Alexandria, although some have questioned the authorship of the latter book (see p. 32). Caesar is justifiably renowned for his various historical writings on events in which he played a leading role (his *Gallic Wars* are probably the most familiar to generations of schoolchildren who studied Latin), but questions of bias and personal self-aggrandizement inevitably arise. Nor do we have in the account of the Alexandrian War personal details about his relationship with Cleopatra. The Roman writer Suetonius (mid-first to mid-second centuries AD) wrote the influential *Life of the Deified Julius* and one of Augustus (the later title of Octavian). His

# Introduction

contemporary, Appian, was an Alexandrian Greek who moved to Rome and wrote in Greek a history of Rome. Parts of this work are often called the *Civil Wars* and cover the turbulent history of the first century BC. The Roman historian Cassius Dio (more commonly known as Dio Cassius) of the mid-second to mid-third century AD wrote eighty books of *Roman History*, also in Greek, of which books 36 to 60 cover the years 69 BC to AD 46.

Probably the most influential ancient writer to shed light on Cleopatra's life and times was the Greek writer Plutarch. He came from a provincial part of Greece, the town of Chaironeia in Boiotia, and lived *c.* AD 50 to 120. Among his voluminous writings is the series *Parallel Lives of the Greeks and Romans*, in which Plutarch paired together biographies of famous figures from Greek and Roman history in order to provide a moral lesson for his readers. Plutarch was self-confessedly and unashamedly writing biography rather than the straight chronological history typified by the writers mentioned above, and he included copious anecdotes (culled from various sources) that he thought illustrated his subjects' characters. His *Life of Caesar* was paired with that of Alexander the

5

Great – an understandable juxtaposition of two great generals – and that of Antony with the life of Demetrius Poliorcetes of Macedon, the brilliant but ultimately feckless and unsuccessful son of one of Alexander the Great's generals. In my opinion, this latter pairing of two such tragic heroes from ancient history shows considerable historical shrewdness on Plutarch's part.

Plutarch's *Lives* were immensely popular in medieval and early modern times, and were widely translated during the Renaissance. Much modern knowledge about figures from classical antiquity derives from them, although scholars have since argued loud and long about their worth as historical sources. Plutarch's *Life of Antony* in particular paints a compelling picture of Cleopatra and Antony, one that has powerfully influenced writers, artists, and film directors of subsequent ages. Shakespeare himself was one who immortalized their love story in his play *Antony and Cleopatra*, based largely on Plutarch. Bernard Shaw's *Caesar and Cleopatra* has also been influential.

Artists from medieval to modern times have found inspiration in various vignettes from the life of Cleopatra (see, for example, plates 5, 6, 11 and

12, and it would be easy enough to produce a lavishly illustrated volume of artists' depictions of her over the centuries. Probably the majority of people in the western world during the twentieth century have seen one or more of the famous film versions of Cleopatra's life, but these bear only a passing resemblance to what historians believe to be the truth. These films have of course had a powerful effect upon popular imagination and have largely determined modern perceptions of her. To fuel this public fascination about Cleopatra, numerous biographies have been written and are still being produced, both serious scholarly works and fanciful fluff based upon unsupported speculation. Recently, too, Cleopatra has been hijacked by the politically correct feminist movement (see Chapter Seven). This book will not be the last in the long line of biographies, but it attempts to describe the life of Cleopatra VII in her historical context, based upon the ancient sources. Given the relative paucity of this evidence, the picture of Cleopatra that will emerge is one which is limited and far less colourful than the works of fiction and film. It is, however, one that I believe to be supported by historical facts.

# HISTORICAL
# BACKGROUND

How did Egypt become Greek, and what were the background events that led to Cleopatra's starring role on the Mediterranean stage? Given that several volumes would be needed for a comprehensive survey of these topics, this brief chapter can only begin to skim over the major issues and will by necessity be highly selective. The study of the three centuries following the death of Alexander the Great in 323 BC is known as 'Hellenistic history', and includes the history of Egypt during that period. A short historical excursus is essential for understanding the Egypt of Cleopatra.

The great native civilization of ancient Egypt had continued, with various vicissitudes, largely unchanged down into the first millennium BC. By the seventh century BC, roughly contemporary with

the period of Greek expansion in the vibrant age
known as the 'archaic period', a Greek colony had
been founded in the Nile Delta at Naucratis, and the
later pharaohs recognized the economic potential of
trading relations with Greece and Phoenicia, a
maritime nation occupying the territory of modern
Israel and Lebanon. However, the Persian Empire of
Asia (comprising modern Turkey, Iraq, Iran, and
lands further east) was the greatest power of its day
and influenced the balance of power in the
Mediterranean for several centuries. In 526 BC the
Great King of Persia, Cambyses, invaded and
conquered Egypt, adding it to the vast lands of his
empire. (The growth of the Persian Empire is
memorably described in the *Histories* of the Greek
historian Herodotus.) Persian rule appears not to
have been popular, with revolts during the fifth
century BC and a long period of independence
during the fourth, but in 343 BC Egypt was
reconquered and became again an uneasy part of the
Persian Empire.

When Alexander the Great of Macedon made his
great expedition into Asia in 334 BC, his pretext was
ostensibly to liberate the Greek cities along the west
coast of Asia Minor that had fallen under Persian

rule. His further aim came to be the defeat and destruction of the Persian Empire, and, in the next years, Alexander conquered the various Persian strongholds that stood in his path. His attention was drawn to Egypt as part of the Persian Empire, and he invaded and conquered the country in 332 BC. Evidence suggests that Alexander was welcomed as a liberator from the hated Persian rule. While in the country, Alexander made the first and indisputedly the greatest of his city-foundations on the Mediterranean coast, on the western (Canopic) branch of the Nile River Delta, naming the city Alexandria after himself. The foundation of the city, with the founder himself allegedly deciding on the layout, walls, and buildings, is well attested in our sources for Alexander. This city was to be his outward-looking capital, whereas the old dynastic capital had been at Memphis, far inland and south of modern Cairo. Alexander's motives for the city-foundation are unclear, but Alexandria certainly had a magnificent location on the coast, and its potential for international trade was soon realized. Alexander retraced his steps east through Egypt and Phoenicia, and journeyed on across the eastern territories of the Persian Empire as far as India. He died in

Babylon in 323 BC while travelling back to the west, and only returned to his first city in his coffin. Though he was temporarily buried at Memphis, Alexander's final resting place was in the city to which he had given his name, at the magnificent tomb known in Greek as the 'Sema'.

When Alexander departed Egypt the new Alexandria had been left under the control of a financial administrator, and appears to have functioned as a city from quite early on. When Alexander died and his empire was divided for purposes of administration among his generals, Egypt passed into the control of Ptolemy the son of Lagus, a Macedonian boyhood friend of Alexander who had served him during the course of the campaign. It was Ptolemy who cunningly diverted Alexander's funeral cortège to Egypt as it was en route to Macedonia. The country remained firmly under his control throughout the turmoil of the power struggles of the next twenty years, and Ptolemy by and large remained aloof from the greed and ambitions for land and power that afflicted Alexander's other generals. All of his policies supported his clear wish for independence from the other 'successors'. Settlers from Greece and

Macedonia were actively encouraged, and Alexandria and other cities in Egypt grew with the influx of a new ruling class. Ptolemy declared himself 'king' in 305 BC, and was styled King Ptolemy I Soter ('Saviour') of Egypt.

Ptolemy established a kingdom in Egypt that was ruled by himself and his direct descendants until the death of Cleopatra VII in 30 BC, whereupon Egypt lost her independence and became a province of Rome. There were fifteen kings of that name – hence the use of the term 'Ptolemaic' to describe this Graeco-Macedonian kingdom in Egypt. Ptolemy and his immediate successors turned their capital Alexandria into a glittering city that became the jewel of the Mediterranean both economically and culturally. The Athens of mainland Greece and other Greek cities paled in comparison. The third century BC was characterized by three good kings, relatively stable government, and enormous prosperity created by the exploitation of natural resources and by extensive foreign trade. The wealth of Egypt was legendary in descriptions by contemporary writers, and the wonders of its capital were a sight to behold. There was a highly sophisticated and intellectual court life as a direct

result of royal artistic patronage and the
establishment of the world-famous Library and
so-called Museum (the word 'mouseion', from
which our word 'museum' derives, means in Greek
a shrine to the Muses, goddesses who were
patronesses of the intellectual arts). The Museum
became a cloistered residence for international
scholars who produced some of the outstanding
literature of Greek antiquity.

Pharos Island marked the approach to
Alexandria's harbours and was originally connected
to the mainland by a bridge dividing the western
from the eastern harbour. The famous Lighthouse of
Alexandria was situated somewhere on this island
and was thus known as the 'Pharos' (see map 2). It
became canonized as one of the Seven Wonders of
the World. The 'Palaces' area, or Royal Quarter,
occupied a substantial part of the ancient city on the
eastern side of the eastern harbour, probably
housing the Library and Museum, the grandiose
palace complexes themselves, and other
establishments such as the Royal Zoo founded by
the second Ptolemy. Outside the Royal Quarter,
wide streets arranged on a rectangular grid system
led past temples, shrines, theatres, the market

place, gymnasia, and all of the standard features found in Greek cities. On the outskirts were extensive necropolis areas with impressive tombs (see pl. 7 for an imaginative reconstruction of Alexandria).

In archaeological terms, Alexandria has suffered the fate of other cities that have been continually inhabited since antiquity, such as Athens or Rome. Excavation has been sporadic and dependent upon the chance availability of areas for exploration. Furthermore, the shoreline has subsided considerably since antiquity (underwater remains have always been clearly visible in the eastern harbour), and in the nineteenth century the construction of the coastal boulevard known as the 'Corniche' caused incalculable damage to the archaeological remains in that area. As I write, spectacular new finds from the ancient city are being made by teams of underwater archaeologists in the eastern harbour, and substantial remains from the Pharos and the Palaces have been recovered. The brief preliminary reports currently available are tantalizing, but it is far too soon for these discoveries to have been fully studied and assessed. The least that can be said is that this work will radically alter our knowledge of the capital of the Ptolemies, and that the potential significance of these current investigations cannot be overestimated. Depending upon the date of the various recovered structures, it is not impossible that a considerable part of the Alexandria of Cleopatra VII has been discovered and will be brought again to daylight.

During the last three centuries BC, the Ptolemaic Empire of Egypt and its possessions co-existed alongside two other Graeco-Macedonian powers, the Seleucid Empire of greater Syria (which comprised most of the Middle East, Iraq, Iran, and lands to the east), and the Antigonid Empire of Macedonia and mainland Greece. Various smaller states controlled parts of Greece and Asia Minor. Warfare was frequent, especially over borders, but a general stability prevailed throughout the third century BC until an additional player emerged upon the Mediterranean stage: Rome. Rome's expansion during this period inevitably clashed with eastern interests and brought her into the orbit of the Hellenistic kingdoms. Rome's eventual domination and ultimate destruction of the Greek East is a huge topic, and is not our business here. But wars were fought with Rome over disputed territory and threatening behaviour (on both sides), and the Hellenistic kings formed shifting alliances both with and against Rome depending upon the perceived advantages to be gained. As Rome gradually conquered Illyria (Albania and parts of the former Yugoslavia), the Macedonian kingdom, and mainland Greece, the eastern powers can have been in no doubt that Rome was now a serious arbiter of Greek affairs.

The dynastic complexities within the Hellenistic powers added fuel to this fire. Large royal families with disaffected or disinherited brothers and sons opened the way for conflict over the succession. Serial marriages of kings with princesses of different nationalities led to rival queens supporting the claims of their own children, and to the possibility of foreign intervention to back up their claims. Also, illegitimate children caused a potential threat as pretenders to the throne. Because of her military strength, Rome was repeatedly invoked on one or the other side of dynastic disputes, meaning that pro- and anti-Roman factions in the empires squabbled with each other, and that Roman puppets were installed and supported upon the Hellenistic thrones at various times.

Ptolemaic Egypt experienced many of these vicissitudes. The first Queen Cleopatra was in fact a Seleucid princess who was married to Ptolemy V at the beginning of the second century BC to cement a peace treaty between Egypt and Syria. After this, things started to go seriously wrong. Successive jealous Ptolemies sequentially warred among themselves and collateral relatives, reunited, ruled jointly, intermarried with their siblings (a Ptolemaic practice going back to the early third century BC, which may have had adverse genetic effects), produced children from incestuous marriages, murdered each other, and appealed to Rome. Fraternal civil wars, exile, incest, and even matricide are well-documented features of second-century Egypt. The result was that the kingdom was weakened and vulnerable to outside interests. The detailed dynastic history of this period is complex in the extreme, and no strong king emerged to stop the rot. Meanwhile, the population of Alexandria had become disgusted with the dynastic debacle and increasingly took power into its own hands through mob rule.

This sets the stage for the birth in 69 BC of Cleopatra, who would become the seventh Ptolemaic queen of that name. Her father was Ptolemy XII Neos Dionysus ('the New Dionysus'), also known as Auletes ('Fluteplayer', a nickname that reflected his frivolous tendencies). Significantly, either Cleopatra's great uncle, Ptolemy X, or his son Ptolemy XI, had bequeathed the kingdom of Egypt to Rome in his will. For the final fifty years of Ptolemaic history, therefore, Egypt's destiny was inextricably entwined with that of Rome.

# THE EARLY YEARS

It has been stated in Chapter One that very little is known about Cleopatra except that which is recorded in our sources for Roman history. She is almost a nonentity until that point in history when she is cast into the orbit of men whose deeds were thought worthy of recording by the ancient historians. It is true that the Romans had political and economic dealings with Egypt throughout the second half of the second century BC and the first half of the first, and therefore the dynastic upheavals of the Ptolemaic royal house are alluded to in our Roman sources, but there was little interest in Cleopatra as an individual (rather than as one of many eastern monarchs, known only in name, who might become a puppet of Rome) until her liaison with Marc Antony. Their potential dynastic liaison, combined with the dangerous political situation in Rome after the murder of Julius Caesar, catapulted the Egyptian queen into the limelight, with the consequence that there is far more information about the end of her life than there is about the beginning. Cleopatra becomes a major figure in Plutarch's *Life of Antony* and other sources that deal with the civil war between him and Octavian. But of her early years we know almost nothing.

## Cleopatra's Family Background

The questions surrounding Cleopatra's family background are notoriously difficult to answer but are crucial to our interpretation of her line of descent and also her physical appearance (see Chapter Seven). It does not help the reader that opinions have differed and still differ in the scholarly world as to the identification of royal family members with the same name; hence, the regnal numbers conventionally given to the Ptolemaic kings and queens have changed over time, and not all books and genealogical tables, especially older ones, are consistent. The reader should not be discouraged by this since the general outline is clear. The genealogical table reproduced in this volume (see pp. 114–15) is the one that I believe to be the most probable.* We know that Cleopatra's father, Ptolemy XII Auletes, was an illegitimate son of Ptolemy IX. The legitimate succession alternated between Ptolemy IX and his brother Ptolemy X (each ruled for a time, was expelled from Egypt, and was restored to the throne in nightmarishly complicated circumstances), and it then passed to Ptolemy X's son, Ptolemy XI. The relationships within the dynasty were by now hopelessly interwoven because of their practice of brother-sister marriage. Brothers married more than one of their sisters and often their nieces (who, frequently, were themselves offspring of a marriage between that brother's own siblings). It also transpired that princesses were married to several family members in succession. The reappearance of the same women in different places in the family tree is reflected in this genealogical cobweb.

The legitimate line of the male Ptolemies died out with the murder of Ptolemy XI, and Auletes succeeded to the throne in 80 BC. We do not know who his mother was, and there is little artistic

---

* Taken from Bowman, Champlin and Lintott (eds), *The Cambridge Ancient History*, vol. IX, pp. 778–9.

evidence about his physical appearance (a possible marble portrait is shown in plate 2). He married a woman who appears to have been his full sister by the same unknown mother, here styled Cleopatra V Tryphaena ('the Opulent one'). They had a mutual brother, also called Ptolemy, who later became king of Cyprus. There has been endless argument over the number of Auletes's marriages and the children produced. It has been conjectured in some quarters that his daughter Berenike (here IV) was the child of Auletes and Cleopatra V, as was possibly a second daughter called Cleopatra (VI, probably also known as Tryphaena), but that his other children, including the famous Cleopatra (VII), were the children of a second, unknown, wife or concubine (this version of the family tree appears in some books). This is based on a complex argument concerning Cleopatra V's apparent disappearance from papyri after 69 BC, and the gap in age between Berenike, Cleopatra VI, and the other children. But this falls far short of historical proof: there is no reliable ancient source on the matter, and no evidence whatsoever as to the identity of a hypothetical second wife. We may also note that accusations of illegitimacy were never made against Cleopatra VII by later hostile Roman sources, who would, presumably, have been only too happy to use them against her if there had been even a suggestion of dubious descent. On balance, it appears the most probable assumption that Auletes and Cleopatra V Tryphaena had six children together: Berenike V, Cleopatra VI, Cleopatra VII, Arsinoe, Ptolemy XIII and Ptolemy XIV (see Chapter Seven for more discussion of the ramifications of Cleopatra's family background).

## The Historical Situation in Egypt in the First Century BC

Although the political history of these turbulent decades does not strictly speaking form a chapter in the life of Cleopatra VII, enough of the historical situation must be described to enable the reader to understand how and why she came to be catapulted to fame through her associations with celebrated Romans. It has been emphasized that Rome was becoming increasingly involved in the affairs of Egypt during this period, mediating for one claimant or another in the on-going battle for the throne. On his death in 81 BC, either Ptolemy X had bequeathed Egypt and Cyprus (then part of the Egyptian kingdom) to Rome, giving the latter a free hand to intervene in Egyptian affairs, or this was done later by his son. This son, Ptolemy XI, was actually established upon the throne by the Roman dictator Sulla in 80 BC, but soon after murdered his stepmother (to whom he was then married) and was himself murdered a few weeks later by the anti-Roman Alexandrian mob, who resented Rome's interference as well as the murder of their queen. Only then did the illegitimate Auletes succeed to the throne of Alexandria, and his brother, Ptolemy, to that of Cyprus.

## The Reign of Ptolemy XII Auletes

It is easy to see that the position of Auletes was far from secure. It did not go unchallenged by two princes of the Seleucid royal house of Syria whose mother was an Egyptian princess. Although Auletes did much to increase his popularity at home by a spate of temple-building, ultimately his fate depended on the firm support of Rome, and, to this end, he paid a huge sum of money in 59 BC to be formally declared a friend and ally of Rome (a precise phrase that imposed reciprocal obligations on both parties). Cassius Dio says that some of this money had been forcibly collected from the Egyptians. This new status of Roman ally did not protect Auletes from the anger of the Alexandrians, who forced him to flee the country in 58 BC. They were angry both because of his appropriation of their money and because of his lack of objection to Rome's recent annexation of Cyprus (the king's brother, Ptolemy of Cyprus, killed himself in opposition to this exercise of Rome's autocratic action). Dio says that the king refused the Alexandrians' demands that he either order Cyprus to be returned or renounce his alliance with Rome, Auletes fled to his ally.

It has been noted that Roman history of the first century BC involved several upheavals in the change from republic to empire. Although this is a bold over-simplification because of limitations of space, the leading characters on the political stage in Rome will only be dealt with here in so far as they impinge upon the history of Egypt and Cleopatra VII. After the end of the dictatorship of Sulla in 78 BC, power gradually became concentrated in the hands of the so-called 'First Triumvirate' in 60 BC, a tripartite sharing of rule between three generals – Pompey (known as 'the

Great'), Crassus (a wealthy aristocrat), and Julius Caesar (soon to embark on his famous military campaigns in Gaul). Pompey provided refuge for Auletes in Rome. The king was involved with the deaths of several members of an embassy of Alexandrians, who had come to Rome to defend the city against charges against them, and eventually went to Ephesus in Asia Minor.

In addition, the changed situation in Egypt set alarm bells ringing in Rome. Upon the departure of Auletes, the Alexandrians had placed on the throne his eldest daughter Berenike V, associated on the throne with her sister Cleopatra VI (who died after a year or so). It is clear that Berenike needed support desperately, and in due course she married a man named Archelaus, nowadays thought to be a son (real or alleged) of Rome's arch-enemy Mithradates VI of Pontus (against whom both Sulla and Pompey had fought difficult and costly wars). In comparison with such a potential threat to Roman interests, Auletes appeared a better bet as king of Egypt, and his cause became a major political issue in Rome. After various vicissitudes, the king was escorted back to Alexandria from Ephesus in 55 BC by Aulus Gabinius, the Roman governor of Syria (Syria had been made a province of

Rome by Pompey after the end of the Seleucid Empire in 64 BC), encouraged by the promise of another substantial sum of money by Auletes.

Gabinius entered Egypt at Pelusium, a city on the easternmost branch of the Nile on the edge of its Delta, and traditionally the threshold to Egypt. His army, which included the young Marc Antony, defeated the opposing Egyptians, and Archelaus was killed in battle. Auletes was reinstalled upon his throne in Alexandria. He not only murdered his daughter Berenike, but also many of the foremost citizens in order to confiscate their wealth, which he now very much needed. The Alexandrians in time became no fonder of Roman intervention than they had been before, and the final years of the reign of Auletes were marked by unrest. He died in 51 BC, leaving a will that confirmed Rome as the arbiter of affairs in Egypt.

## *The Accession of Cleopatra VII in 51 BC*

It was against this political backdrop that the throne of Egypt fell to Auletes's elder son Ptolemy XIII (a child of ten), and to his eldest remaining daughter Cleopatra VII (now seventeen years old). The two were married in accordance with Ptolemaic custom, but the boy-king as a minor fell under the control of two ministers, a eunuch called Pothinus and the general Achillas. These forceful men established a tight reign over the young Ptolemy, clearly seeing their route to personal political power through a total domination and exploitation of the boy. Consequently they fomented discord between brother and sister and engineered a civil war between them. Cleopatra appears on the world stage for the first time at this period. Even at the age of seventeen she seems to have shown considerable energy and ambition. Sources attest that she went to some lengths to secure support from the native population of Egypt against her brother and his unscrupulous ministers. She achieved this by actively supporting the native religious cults of Egypt as a whole. None the less, Cleopatra was expelled from Alexandria by the combined influence of her brother and his ministers. She went east to Syria to try to muster an army.

Meanwhile, the political situation in Rome did not stand still. The First Triumvirate had ended with the death of Crassus in a catastrophic defeat at Carrhae in Parthia in 53 BC. Pompey and Caesar gradually fell out with each other, and the ambitious Caesar came to be seen as a threat to the republic. Rome was in a state of civil war by 49 BC. The armies of Pompey and Caesar finally met in battle in August 48 BC, on a plain near the town of Pharsalus in Thessaly in central Greece. Pompey's cavalry was routed with severe losses, his remaining troops panicked, and the general himself fled the battlefield. This was a decisive battle in Roman history, since Julius Caesar was now the unopposed power in Rome, and it changed the course of Roman history.

After the defeat at Pharsalus, Pompey fled to Egypt first via the eastern Mediterranean island of Lesbos, and then via Cilicia in southern Asia Minor. Appian and Dio tell us that Pompey was uncertain where to go, but finally settled on Egypt, which was still powerful in ships, provisions, and money. Furthermore, Auletes, the father of the current young rulers, had been Pompey's friend during his lifetime. At this time, Ptolemy XIII's army was mustered at Mount Casius to the east of Pelusium awaiting his sister Cleopatra's expected invasion from Syria. When Pompey's ship appeared offshore and a message was sent to Ptolemy announcing his arrival, the ministers Achillas and Pothinus deliberated what was the best course to take. The sources (Appian and Caesar himself) give various reasons for their decision that Pompey should be killed: fear that Pompey might seize Egypt, disgust at his failing fortunes, or hope that they would win favour from his conqueror Caesar. Although Pompey's suspicions were aroused, he came ashore but was murdered. His head was cut off and saved for Caesar to behold, and his body was buried at the foot of Mount Casius.

Meanwhile, Caesar followed Pompey from Pharsalus along the eastern Mediterranean, and eventually arrived in Alexandria with soldiers and warships. Thus the stage was now set for the fateful meeting between Caesar and Cleopatra.

*F O U R*

# JULIUS CAESAR

The meeting of Caesar (in full Gaius Julius
Caesar) and Cleopatra marked her debut as a
great romantic heroine in modern tradition,
especially since their association was a prelude to
her cataclysmic love affair with Marc Antony. The
ancient sources for the relationship between Caesar
and Cleopatra are not good, but, because of the
elaboration of the few known facts by Bernard Shaw
(in his *Caesar and Cleopatra*) and Hollywood into a
fuller (and therefore more satisfying) story, the
modern world thinks that it knows far more about
this couple than can in fact be supported by the
evidence. It should be remembered that Caesar was
now a man in his early fifties and married to his
third Roman wife, the aristocratic and well-
connected Calpurnia. A marble portrait of Caesar is
shown in plate 3, a head of the second century AD
now in the Museo Nazionale in Napoles. The head
reveals a man of mature years who is losing his hair.

Cleopatra by contrast was just twenty or so years old when they met.

Soon after Caesar's arrival in Egypt, he fought on Cleopatra's behalf the so-called 'Alexandrian War' against her brother Ptolemy XIII, during the winter of 48/47 BC. Caesar wrote an account of the background to this war in Book 3 of his *Civil Wars*. There exists a separate work called the *Alexandrian War* that may or may not have been written by an officer of his called Hirtius (this has been disputed; see p. 4); whoever the author, it is nevertheless written very much from Caesar's point of view. Although these two works offer detailed evidence about the political background and military campaigns of the Alexandrian War, Cleopatra is notable by her absence. In the former work she is only mentioned twice, and in the latter once, in totally matter-of-fact terms as the young queen who was at war with her brother. Perhaps this is not surprising given the nature and purpose of these self-justifying historical works, but the important fact is that we have no evidence from Caesar's viewpoint about any personal relations he had with Cleopatra. We are left to rely on Plutarch in his *Life of Caesar* and Cassius Dio, with a few comments by other ancient sources.

## The Meeting of Caesar and Cleopatra

Upon arrival in Alexandria, Caesar is said to have
wept when presented with the head of his defeated
rival Pompey, and ordered it to be buried. He acted
imperiously in the city and occupied the royal
palace although the Alexandrians agitated against
him, especially when he began to demand money
from the populace in repayment of the old debt of
Auletes. It was allegedly when adverse winds
prevented any departure from Egypt that Caesar
decided to settle the dispute between the young
Ptolemy and his sister Cleopatra, who had re-
entered Egypt and taken up residence somewhere
outside Alexandria.

At some uncertain date, Caesar and Cleopatra
met at the palace in Alexandria. Cassius Dio records
that the queen had at first been in contact with
Caesar by means of her agents who argued her
cause against her brother, but that she later asked to
meet him in person and that the request was
granted. Dio states quite categorically that Caesar's
reputation as a ladies' man had preceded him: '. . .
she discovered his disposition (which was very
susceptible, to such an extent that he had his

intrigues with ever so many other women – with all, doubtless, who chanced to come in his way) . . .' (42.34.3). Cleopatra therefore put her trust in her beauty, her charm, and the brilliance of her conversation to subjugate 'even a love-sated man past his prime' (42.43.5). For the occasion she adorned herself carefully to appear majestic yet deserving of pity. Plutarch preserves the famous anecdote that she came to the palace in secret, although concealed not in a carpet, as depicted in cinematic versions of the story, but rather in a linen sack used for bedding and carried into Caesar's presence by her trusted friend (*Life of Caesar*, 49). Both sources agree that Caesar was immediately captivated by the young queen, and became determined to reconcile her with her brother to preserve her throne.

Apparently to the disgruntlement of young Ptolemy XIII, a temporary but shaky settlement was achieved. This was formalized in a public assembly during which Caesar read out to the populace the will of Auletes that stated that brother and sister should rule in common under the guardianship of the Roman people. In his role as dictator it was in his power to bestow the kingdom on Cleopatra and Ptolemy XIII, and he furthermore gave the island of Cyprus to their younger siblings, Ptolemy (later the XIV) and Arsinoe.

## The Alexandrian War

Any role that Cleopatra may have played during the Alexandrian War is not recorded. Presumably she remained in the palace at Alexandria and in contact with Caesar, but we hear nothing of her until the conclusion of the war. The eunuch Pothinus was furious at Caesar's intervention in the fraternal dispute he had carefully staged, and summoned Ptolemy XIII's army back west to Alexandria and put it under the command of the general Achillas. The odds were not on Caesar's side during the war that broke out, although he retained control of Ptolemy XIII. Caesar had few troops, and ranged against him was a competent army composed largely of Roman ex-soldiers who had served with Gabinius in Syria. The Alexandrians remained hostile as always to Roman interference. Several battles took place on land and sea, and much damage was done to the city. Caesar reports in his *Civil Wars* (3.111) that at a battle in the harbour he was forced to burn the Alexandrian fleet to deny its use to the enemy. He also burned the ships in the dockyards, from where the fire spread and destroyed the grain supplies as well as part of the great Library of Alexandria situated in the Palaces area near the shore. Scholars are uncertain whether the destruction of the Library was partial or total, but it seems that the damage to its contents was severe. The extent of the loss of much ancient Greek literature as a result of this accidental disaster cannot be overestimated. Finally Caesar was able to occupy and fortify the island of Pharos (the site of the famous Lighthouse), thereby regaining control of the harbour. He summoned reinforcements from abroad to his aid.

Cleopatra's otherwise shadowy younger sister Arsinoe now made her one appearance in history, as attested by Caesar and Dio. In collusion with a eunuch named Ganymede, Arsinoe (who with her brother had been given rule in Cyprus) was declared queen by the Alexandrians, and she joined forces with the general Achillas. At this time Pothinus was executed by Caesar, according to Dio out of fear that he might contrive to kidnap Ptolemy XIII, but the murder outraged the Alexandrians even more. They were not appeased even when Caesar had the boy-king speak to the people urging peace, since they assumed it was a plot by the Roman.

Arsinoe and Achillas now headed the opposition, but, as each desired supreme power, a quarrel broke out and Achillas was killed by Ganymede. Arsinoe thereby gained sole control and entrusted the army to Ganymede, who continued to pursue the war vigorously by blocking the city's water supply and engaging in several naval encounters. Caesar's reinforcements from Cilicia and Syria were by now drawing near, approaching Alexandria from Pelusium in the east.

At this point the Alexandrians sent to Caesar asking for the release into their hands of the king Ptolemy XIII, pretending that they wanted to consult with him about possible peace terms. It seems unlikely that they were really seeking terms, but the sources say that the people had already tired of the tyranny of Arsinoe and Ganymede. It is not possible to know who was deceiving whom: Caesar, the boy, and the Alexandrians all apparently thought that they had the upper hand and had fooled the other parties. In any event, Ptolemy was released to the Alexandrians, and he became their figurehead leader in whose name they continued to wage war. In 47 BC a fierce battle was fought east of Alexandria by the Alexandrians against Caesar's recently arrived allies, whom Caesar's forces came to relieve. The battle is described in detail in Caesar's *Alexandrian War*. The Romans were victorious, and King Ptolemy XIII was drowned in the Nile when his escape vessel capsized.

## The Aftermath of the War

For a second time Caesar was the arbiter of political affairs in Alexandria, and Cleopatra now reappears in history. In an attempt to justify his actions for posterity, Caesar himself is splendidly economical with the truth, recording only that he assigned the kingdom to the younger Ptolemy (XIV) and to Cleopatra (VII) in accordance with the will of their father, and that he had their rebellious sister Arsinoe 'removed from the kingdom' (*Alexandrian War*, 33). (She was later dragged from her sanctuary at Ephesus and killed on the orders of Marc Antony.) Caesar gives the distinct impression that he left Alexandria immediately afterwards, leaving three Roman legions to support the new rulers. The other sources, however, give a much more circumstantial account and concentrate on the personal aspects of the relationship between Caesar and Cleopatra.

Dio states unequivocally that Caesar bestowed the kingdom upon Cleopatra alone, since he had waged the war for her sake. His words will suffice:

> Yet, being afraid that the Egyptians might rebel again, because they were delivered over to a woman to rule, and that the Romans might be angry, both on this account and because he was living with the woman, he commanded her to 'marry' her other brother, and gave the kingdom to both of them, at least nominally. For in reality Cleopatra was to hold all the power alone, since her husband was still a boy, and in view of Caesar's favour there was nothing that she could not do. Hence her living with her brother and sharing the rule with him was a mere pretence which she accepted, whereas in truth she ruled alone and spent her time in Caesar's company. (42.44.2–4)

## Caesar and Cleopatra Together

It was apparently at this time that Caesar and Cleopatra took their Nile cruise that has passed into legend. Appian says that four hundred of Caesar's ships sailed up the Nile so that he could explore Egypt with

Cleopatra and generally enjoy himself with her (*Civil Wars*, vol. 3, bk 2, 90). He states that the details of these events are related in more detail in his history of Egypt, but, maddeningly, this work is lost. Suetonius talks of feasting until dawn, and relates that the cruise was made in her state barge (a river-going ship called a thalamegos), and that they would have gone as far as Ethiopia except that his soldiers refused to follow (*Life of the Deified Julius*, 52). But we know no more than this, and must imagine any details.

Caesar left Egypt sometime during 47 BC (the length of time he spent idling with Cleopatra is unknown and disputed), leaving Cleopatra on the throne. He went off to campaign in Asia Minor against the forces of Pharnaces of Pontus, son of Rome's old enemy Mithradates VI. Dio suggests that the pair would have stayed together in Egypt longer or would have set out together for Rome were it not for this war, but it is not clear what his evidence is for such an assertion. By now Cleopatra was pregnant, and in the course of the year 47 BC she gave birth to a son whom the Alexandrians called Caesarion ('Little Caesar').

The paternity of this child has been disputed although the ancient sources accept that Caesar was the father. Octavian (Caesar's adopted son) denied that this was true, but his vested interest in so doing is evident. Suetonius says that Caesar allowed Cleopatra to give the baby his own name, and that certain Greek writers attested that the boy was very like Caesar. According to Suetonius, Marc Antony (Caesar's loyal supporter) told the Roman senate that Caesar had acknowledged the child, but, again, Antony's vested interest in so doing is clear, given his rivalry with Octavian. But not all in Rome believed that Caesarion was Caesar's child. The use of the name, however, probably signifies that Caesar himself at least believed that the child was his. On the Egyptian side, however, Cleopatra clearly regarded the birth of her son with great importance, since she issued coinage depicting herself holding the infant.

Caesar returned to Rome after defeating Pharnaces, and celebrated four triumphs, one of which was in honour of his Egyptian victory in the Alexandrian War. Cleopatra is not named in the context of the various triumphal processions, but we are told that he built a temple to Venus (from whom the Julian family claimed descent), in accordance with his vow before the battle against

Pompey at Pharsalus, and placed a beautiful statue
of Cleopatra next to that of the goddess. Appian says
that it stood there in his own day (*Civil Wars*, vol. 3,
bk 2, 102). If this can be believed then he had
evidently not forgotten Cleopatra, although he had
returned to Rome and, presumably, to Calpurnia.

In 46 BC Cleopatra and her child followed Caesar
to Rome. Her reasons for doing so are unclear,
although Suetonius implies that Caesar summoned
her. The truth of this is unknown, but Dio implies that
her presence in the city was not welcomed by all:

> . . . he [Caesar] incurred the greatest censure from all
> because of his passion for Cleopatra – not now the
> passion he had displayed in Egypt (for that was a
> matter of hearsay), but that which was displayed in
> Rome itself. For she had come to the city with her
> husband and settled in Caesar's own house, so that he
> too derived an ill repute on account of both of them.
> He was not at all concerned, however, about this, but
> actually enrolled them among the friends and allies of
> the Roman people. (43.27.3)

One can well imagine the reaction of Calpurnia to
Cleopatra's presence (could she really have been
installed in the *same* house, or in a different one that

Caesar had bought for her?), but Dio's comment makes it clear that Caesar's visible liaison with the queen severely compromised his standing and reputation in Rome. That he ran roughshod over public feeling can hardly have helped his popularity. (For more speculation about Cleopatra's motives in coming to Rome, see Chapter Seven.)

It is noteworthy, however, that there is no mention of the child Caesarion in the will that Caesar drew up on 13 September 45 BC (Suetonius, *The Deified Julius*, 83) At this period Cleopatra and her son were resident in Rome, but Caesar made posthumous provision for adopting his great-nephew Octavian and giving him his name, Crucially, he appointed guardians for any son who might still be born to him. The implication can only be that in 45 BC he was still hoping to have a child with his legal wife Calpurnia. Whether Cleopatra knew it or not, Caesar did not make Caesarion one of his heirs at Rome. The different views each had of their child's official place are striking, and one wonders how the situation might have developed had Caesar lived for several more years.

The two years Cleopatra spent in Rome coincided with serious developments in the political life of the city, which have themselves been the subject of countless books. Caesar continued to wield supreme power in his campaigns abroad and received extravagant honours at Rome, leading to accusations among some that he had destroyed the republic, aspired to divinity, and intended to declare himself king. A conspiracy was hatched against him by disaffected nobles, the result of which is known to every schoolchild. Gaius Julius Caesar was murdered in the Roman Senate on the Ides of March (March 15) in 44 BC. Any dreams that Cleopatra may have had for a future with the man who had been her champion and protector for eleven years were shattered, along with any notions that she and Caesarion had found safety in Rome.

# MARC ANTONY

The civil war that followed Caesar's murder changed the course of Roman history, and its victor became the first emperor of Rome. These major historical events cannot be considered in any detail in a book of this type, and perhaps this chapter will continue the sensation of viewing history from the sidelines. However, the romance of Antony and Cleopatra was played out against this grander backdrop, and in a work that concentrates on Cleopatra, their relationship functions as a window through which we glimpse, darkly, the larger historical picture. Plutarch's *Life of Antony* naturally emphasizes their romance, but it was actually peripheral to other events happening at the time, at least until the couple's last days in Alexandria.

After Caesar's assassination, Cleopatra and Caesarion returned to Alexandria. No details are recorded about what must have been a hugely traumatic and potentially dangerous situation for the queen alone in Rome following his murder. After her return, she ordered the murder of her younger brother and husband, Ptolemy XIV, which meant that she was the sole surviving child of Ptolemy Auletes in Egypt and now the uncontested occupant of the throne. Significantly, she associated her young son Caesarion with her on the throne as Ptolemy XV. The importance she attached to the child has already been mentioned regarding her issue of her coinage depicting mother and baby on the obverse. He continued to be publicly depicted with her, especially in Egyptianizing guise presumably intended to appeal to the native subjects (plate 4 shows Cleopatra and Caesarion as the Egyptian gods Isis and Horus on a relief from the Ptolemaic Temple of Hathor at Dendara in Upper Egypt).

## *The Early Life of Marc Antony*

A thumbnail historical sketch is needed to explain how Marc Antony's path crossed that of Cleopatra. Marcus Antonius was probably born in 83 BC, and after an allegedly dissipated youth, became a

Roman soldier. It has been mentioned in the last chapter that he served under Aulus Gabinius in Syria (as a cavalry commander), and that, in this capacity, he was one of the troops who escorted Cleopatra's father Ptolemy Auletes back to his throne in Alexandria in 55 BC. Antony distinguished himself in the various battles that were fought as part of this invasion of Egypt, and he received credit for the fitting burial of Archelaus (the husband of Cleopatra's elder sister Berenike IV, against whom they were fighting). Plutarch says that he left Alexandria with a very high reputation, but it is not certain if he met, saw, or even knew about the fourteen-year-old Cleopatra on this visit (only Appian says that he met and fell in love with her back then (*Civil Wars*, vol. 4, bk 5, 8)). By this time Antony had already embarked on his own marital career. He had had a liaison with a woman called Fadia, and at this time was married to his cousin Antonia. (A portrait coin of Antony is shown in plate 10.)

Antony went on to become a trusted friend and general of Julius Caesar. He served with him in Gaul, and held various offices in Rome, as one would expect of a young nobleman ascending the political ladder in the usual way. As the drama of the First Triumvirate unfolded, Antony defended Caesar's interests and was left in charge of Italy when Caesar was fighting in Spain. He took part on Caesar's side at the Battle of Pharsalus against Pompey in 48 BC, commanding one wing of the army. He and Caesar were consuls together at Rome in the fateful year 44 BC. It has been stated in the last chapter that many Romans suspected that Caesar intended to declare himself king. These suspicions were no doubt fuelled by one remarkable incident during the festival of the Lupercalia in 44 BC, in which Marc Antony was involved; the latter offered a diadem (a symbol of royalty) to Caesar. It was a tense moment, but Caesar declined it.

After Caesar's death, Antony naturally became one of the leading 'pro-Caesarians' who were determined to avenge the murder. Significantly, Antony presided over Caesar's emotional funeral, and gave a memorable funeral eulogy that is attested in many ancient sources (Plutarch, Cassius Dio, Appian, Suetonius, and the orator Cicero; their descriptions were elaborated by Shakespeare into several speeches culminating in the famous oration beginning: 'Friends, Romans, countrymen, lend me your ears' ( *Julius Caesar*, III, ii, 74)).

After various political manoeuvrings and internecine struggles within the pro-Caesarian party, the Second Triumvirate was finally formed in 43 BC to restore the state. Its members were Antony, Caesar's great-nephew and posthumously adopted son Octavian, and Marcus Lepidus. Their main enemies were two of Caesar's assassins, Brutus and Cassius, who were eventually defeated by Antony and Octavian in 42 BC at the Battle of Philippi in eastern Macedonia near the boundary with Thrace. In the subsequent agreement made with Octavian, Antony agreed to reorganize the eastern half of Roman territory while Octavian received the west. This put Antony in charge of the wealthy eastern provinces, which of course included Egypt under the control of its queen Cleopatra VII. As the triumvir Lepidus gradually faded from the picture, Antony and Octavian became the main protagonists on the Roman stage, and their increasing suspicions of, and consequent alienation from, each other led to the major civil war between them to which I have often referred. This is the background to the final eleven years of Cleopatra's life.

## The Meeting of Antony and Cleopatra
### in 41 BC

Marc Antony was in Cilicia, an area on the south-eastern coast of modern Turkey, en route to a war in Parthia, when he summoned Cleopatra to meet him to answer charges that she had abetted his old enemy Cassius in the civil war. Plutarch makes a great deal of this meeting, using it, after a long digression on Antony's character, to mark the beginning of his decline: '. . . now as a crowning evil his love for Cleopatra supervened, roused and drove to frenzy many of the passions that were still hidden and quiescent in him, and dissipated and destroyed whatever good and saving qualities still offered resistance' (*Life of Antony*, 25.1). Although Plutarch presents Cleopatra as Antony's fatal flaw from the moment of their meeting, and him as a crazed slave to love, we must take this with a pinch of salt. In 47 BC Antony had divorced his wife Antonia, and shortly thereafter married a (by all accounts) formidable and well-connected woman named Fulvia, who was alive until 40 BC and was an important factor in his political life since she looked after his interests in Rome during his absence.

Cleopatra sailed to meet Antony, apparently cunningly calculating the effect of her beauty and presence upon him. 'For Caesar and Pompey had known her when she was still a girl and inexperienced in affairs, but she was going to visit Antony at the very time when women have most brilliant beauty and are at the acme of intellectual power' (*Life of Antony*, 25.3). She travelled to Cilicia in her barge (probably a thalamegos from her fleet of river-going vessels, which could have hugged the coast as far as Cilicia), and sailed up the Cydnus River to the town of Tarsus. (Tarsus is about 30 kilometres east of the modern Turkish town of Mersin, and was later to be the home town of St Paul, born Saul of Tarsus, 'a citizen of no mean city'(Acts 21:39).) Plutarch's description cannot be bettered, and formed the basis of Shakespeare's depiction of the scene. Cleopatra arrived

> in a barge with a gilded poop, its sails spread purple, its rowers urging it on with silver oars to the sound of the flute blended with pipes and lutes. She herself reclined beneath a canopy spangled with gold, adorned like Venus in a painting, while boys like Loves in paintings stood on either side and fanned her. Likewise also the fairest of her serving-maidens,

attired like Nereids and Graces, were stationed, some at the rudder-sweeps, and others at the reefing-ropes. Wondrous odours from countless incense-offerings diffused themselves along the river-banks. Of the inhabitants, some accompanied her on either bank of the river from its very mouth, while others went down from the city to behold the site. The throng in the market-place gradually streamed away, until at last Antony himself, seated on his tribunal, was left alone. And a rumour spread on every hand that Venus was come to revel with Bacchus for the good of Asia. (*Life of Antony*, 26.2–3)

Many scholars have argued that we can accept this charming picture as largely true in substance if not in every detail (see plate 5 for a highly imaginative modern interpretation of the arrival of Cleopatra on her barge). Cleopatra had nothing to lose and everything to gain by making a favourable impression on Antony. If he were now to be the Roman arbiter of affairs in the east, Cleopatra needed his support. The effect that such an unexpected, dramatic appearance at Tarsus must have had on Antony can only be imagined, and Cassius Dio and Appian support Plutarch's view that the Roman was instantly smitten. Cleopatra invited him to a sumptuous banquet aboard her barge, and was entertained by him the following day (the feasts between the pair are popular subjects of later paintings).

Despite the threatening political situation, Antony spent the following winter with the queen in Alexandria. Plutarch describes in detail the louche life they led together, allegedly based on evidence from a physician who was at court at the time and knew Plutarch's grandfather (*Life of Antony*, 28ff.). They formed a dining society called 'The Inimitable Livers', which feasted everyday in indescribable extravagance. Antony and Cleopatra spent the rest of their time together drinking, hunting, fishing, playing dice, and talking. The charms of Cleopatra and the allure of eastern delights clearly appealed to Antony's nature. She bore him twins the following year in 40 BC: a boy named Alexander Helios ('Sun'), and a girl named Cleopatra Selene ('Moon').

### The Years Leading to Actium

The events of the next few years, however, argue strongly that, at this stage anyway, Antony's head still ruled his heart. He left Egypt to deal with political developments in Italy, and he made an agreement with Octavian that was cemented by marriage to Octavian's half-sister Octavia. There is no evidence that he saw Cleopatra for some years, until he returned to the east in 37 BC. Because our sources concentrate on his involvement in political affairs in Italy, Syria and Parthia, Cleopatra falls out of our picture, except for references to generous grants of territory he made her. One may wonder, after a winter of such delights, what Cleopatra made of Antony's absence and the news of his remarriage to such an important woman now that she was the mother of two of his children. What was Antony up to? Had their affair been mere fun and infatuation, was he really in love but genuinely kept away by events, or did he feel that public support of Cleopatra, a determined monarch with a wealthy kingdom, was a shrewd move as far as his policy in the east was concerned? It must be noted that elsewhere in the east Antony ruled through client-kings who were loyal to Rome. Perhaps he saw Cleopatra in this role.

Antony returned to the east in the company of Octavia in 39 BC, but on his next trip in 37 BC (his departure was the last time he saw Italy or

1. Marble portrait head of Cleopatra VII. (Antikensammlung, Staatliche Museen zu Berlin – Preussischer Kulturbesitz – Ingrid Geske-Heiden)

2. Marble portrait head of Ptolemy XII Auletes (?), father of Cleopatra VII. (Ma 3449 @ photographie Musée du Louvre – Patrick Lebaube)

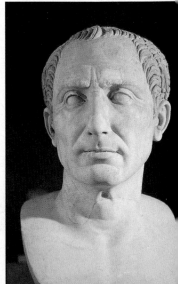

3. Second-century AD marble portrait head of Julius Caesar from the Museo Nazionale, Naples. (Photo: Bridgeman Art Library, London)

4.   Egyptianizing depiction of Cleopatra and Caesarion as Isis and Horus from the
Ptolemaic Temple of Hathor at Denderah in Upper Egypt. (Photo: Peter Clayton)

5. Artist's romantic view of Cleopatra: William Etty, *Arrival of Cleopatra*. (The Board of Trustees of the National Museums and Galleries on Merseyside)

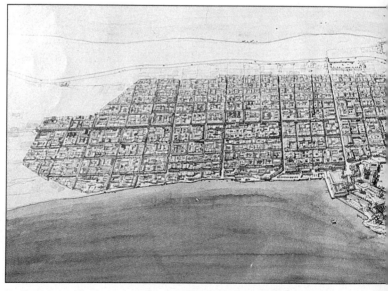

7. Imaginative reconstruction of ancient Alexandria, seen from the north. (S. Compoint/Sygma)

6. Artist's romantic view of Cleopatra: Lawrence Alma-Tadema, *Antony and Cleopatra*, 1883. (Photo: Bridgeman Art Library, London)

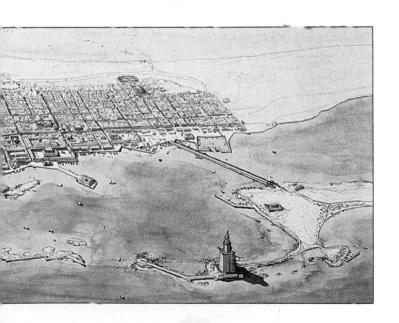

Two coin portraits of Cleopatra
VII: 8. left: 'Hellenistic' type
(Photo: Peter Clayton);
9. below: 'Romanized' type
(Photo: Peter Clayton)

10. Coin portrait of
Marc Antony. (Photo:
Peter Clayton)

11. Depiction of the meeting between Cleopatra and Octavian, by Louis Gauffier, 1787–8. (National Galleries of Scotland / Photo: Bridgeman Art Library, London)

12.   Depiction of the death of Cleopatra by John Collier. (© Oldham Art Gallery: Oldham MBC Museums Service/Photo: Bridgeman Art Library, London)

Octavian) his wife was left behind, and Cleopatra met him in Syria. Again, Plutarch attributes this to unbridled passion on Antony's part: 'But the dire evil which had been slumbering for a long time, namely, his passion for Cleopatra, which men thought had been charmed away and lulled to rest by better considerations, blazed up again with renewed power as he drew near Syria' (*Life of Antony*, 36.1). Her kingdom was again increased by further grants of territory. It is often claimed that at this stage Antony and Cleopatra were 'married', but clearly this could not have been technically possible in Roman eyes because of his existing legal marriage to Octavia, regardless of what Egyptians might have thought about such a double 'marriage'. Yet it seems evident that their relationship now stood on a more solid basis, since Antony acknowledged his paternity of their twins. Cleopatra bore him another son the following year, Ptolemy Philadelphus, the same name and epithet of arguably the greatest Ptolemaic king of the dynasty, Ptolemy II Philadelphus, under whom Egypt had reached the pinnacle of fame and prosperity in the third century BC. The choice of name must have been deliberate.

Plutarch says that these actions caused enormous offence at Rome, but that Antony brushed objections aside, saying that 'noble families were extended by the successive begettings of many kings' (*Life of Antony*, 36.3–4). Scholars have wondered why Antony acted in such a reckless manner, since he now had much to lose. His rival Octavian was a master of propaganda and Antony must have realized that such an insult to his sister would be a public relations disaster for Antony back home in Italy. None the less, he went ahead with an explicit acknowledgement of Cleopatra's position in his life. One might be tempted to agree with Plutarch that Antony was now infatuated beyond all reason, which indeed seems to be the easiest explanation, but it cannot be the whole story since Antony left Cleopatra soon afterwards for a war of unspecified length in Parthia and Armenia (Plutarch says brusquely that he sent Cleopatra back to Egypt). Perhaps his reasoning was political, if misjudged. If he really *was* consciously trying to strengthen his position as a ruler in the eastern style, for the benefit of eastern client-kings in an empire that was rapidly becoming divided between east and west, his strategy backfired at Rome. We may note in this context plate 9, which shows a coin minted by Antony with his head on one side, and with Cleopatra's on the other. This juxtaposition shows Cleopatra very much in the role of a client-king of the Roman Empire, and the depiction of her is very much in a Roman style, for consumption outside of Egypt. (For further discussion of this portrait, see Chapter Seven.) If Antony was becoming 'easternized' for public consumption, he contrived to make Cleopatra seem equally 'westernized'.

Antony's invasion of Parthia was a disaster, with the loss of more than 20,000 men. The sorry tale is described in detail in Plutarch. In the winter of 36 BC Antony was in a hurry to escape the severe winter weather of inland Asia and awaited Cleopatra in Phoenicia. Plutarch marks his decline: '. . . and since she was slow in coming he was beside himself with distress, promptly resorting to drinking and intoxication, although he could not hold out long at table, but in the midst of the drinking would often rise or spring up to look out, until she put into port . . .' (*Life of Antony*, 51.2).

In 35 BC Antony invaded Armenia but turned back when he heard the news that his wife Octavia had decided to journey east to him with troops, money and supplies (it is not clear if she was put up to this by her brother Octavian, who sensed an opportunity to embarrass Antony severely). Antony's discomfiture was considerable, but he accepted the gift, either ordering Octavia to stay behind in Athens (Plutarch) or to return to Rome (Dio). It has been argued that Octavia would hardly have travelled east to help Antony unless she still considered herself his wife. When she finally returned to Rome, Plutarch says that she went back to her husband's house, cared for his children, and carried on her normal life. Her exemplary behaviour made Antony even more unpopular in Rome.

Antony then spent the winter of 35/34 BC with Cleopatra in Alexandria. Plutarch includes a digression on Cleopatra's supposed conduct once she had been threatened by the proximity of Octavia. She '*pretended* [my italics] to be passionately in love with Antony' (*Life of Antony*, 53), gazing at him rapturously when he was present and falling into melancholy when he departed, and weeping 'surreptitiously', while hoping to be noticed. It is not clear whether this is Plutarch's gratuitous description of stereotyped feminine coquettish wiles, which he thought suited the situation, or if it is based on good evidence.

During the campaigning season of 34 BC, Antony again invaded Armenia and by guile captured the renegade king Artavasdes. He was conveyed back to Alexandria as a prisoner, and a huge procession was staged, marred only by the refusal of the Armenian prisoners to pay public homage to Cleopatra. This type of celebration was uncomfortably close to a traditional Roman triumph, transferred to a foreign shore. The pro-Octavian party must have been horrified, and their resulting propaganda hugely damaging to Antony. Even worse was the ceremony traditionally called 'the Donations of Alexandria', which may or may not have been held on the same occasion.

At a spectacle in the gymnasium of Alexandria, golden thrones were placed on a dais for Antony and Cleopatra (dressed as the new Isis), with lower ones for their sons. Antony declared Cleopatra Queen of Egypt, Cyprus, Libya, and Syria in association with her son Caesarion. Their own sons were acclaimed King of Kings; Alexander Helios was granted Armenia, Media and Parthia, and Ptolemy Philadelphus Phoenicia, Syria, and Cilicia. The boys were paraded in the ethnic costumes of these regions, and received national bodyguards

(Plutarch, *Life of Antony*, 53; Dio, 49.40–41). This claim of dynastic succession combined with the grant of existing Roman provinces to foreign princelings was too much for Antony's enemies, and war with Octavian was now inevitable.

## The Battle of Actium*

The propaganda war intensified and Antony and his supporters were gradually ostracized by the Roman establishment. He gathered together a great contingent of allied forces in the east, and mustered them at Ephesus in Ionia. Egypt supplied huge numbers of warships, merchant ships, supplies and generous funds, which meant that Cleopatra was indispensable to the operation in economic and military terms regardless of what anyone on Antony's side might have thought in private. The fleet headed west, stopping at Samos. Plutarch gives a detailed description of the merrymaking that took place there, which clearly echoed the extravagance of their first winter together in Alexandria (*Life of Antony*, 56–7). In 32 BC Antony finally divorced Octavia,

---

\*    For a full account of this battle see Carter, *The Battle of Actium*.

perhaps believing that less damage would be done than if she divorced him first, as she surely would have had to do once he went to war with her brother.

Not to be outdone, Octavian illegally took Antony's will away from the Vestal Virgins in Rome and made the contents public to the senate. Whether or not this was the real will, or one devised by Octavian to inflame the situation, the provisions included a request that Antony's body be sent to Cleopatra for burial in Egypt. After further political manoeuvring, Octavian had Antony stripped of his remaining official powers, and war declared on Cleopatra. Anyone who sided with her would also be deemed an enemy of Rome. Rome had in effect declared war on Antony.

By the winter of 32/31 BC Antony's allied fleet and land forces had moved westward into mainland Greece and had gathered on the west coast with the main naval concentration at the Actium promontory on the south shore of the entrance to the Ambracian Gulf. (The modern town of Preveza lies on the northern side of the entrance of this gulf, where Antony's second camp was established.) Antony's forces were numerically superior both on land and sea to those of Octavian, and his position was a good one, but it all went very wrong. Instead of attacking Octavian's fleet as it sailed across from Italy, Antony allowed the harbours of western Greece to be occupied by Octavian's forces, which was a major tactical error. Moreover, various land skirmishes were lost by Antony's allies, and many troops deserted to Octavian. Antony was in effect blockaded at Actium both by land and sea, even as his force was afflicted by disease and lack of water and supplies.

The major battle took place on 2 September 31 BC, with Octavian's fleet lined up off shore and Antony's by now diminished fleet facing it with their sterns to the land. Cleopatra's ships formed a line behind those of Antony across the entrance to the gulf. Nothing happened until both lines began to drift apart from north to south and gaps appeared. To the astonishment of all, Cleopatra's ships took advantage of this, hoisted sail, and broke out through a gap in Octavian's line. The blockade was thereby successfully broken, but it is not clear what Cleopatra was doing, or what Antony thought she was doing. Was she cunningly trying to escape the blockade in order to perform an outflanking manoeuvre, or was she fleeing the scene, leaving

Antony and his ships to their fate (the latter has been alleged since warships did not normally carry sails into battle)? In any event, Antony followed her, leaving his flagship for a smaller, faster vessel, and transferred to her flagship. Why did he do this? Seeing Antony's departure, the rest of his fleet lost heart, and there does not seem to have been much actual fighting.

The Battle of Actium, so crucial to the course of Roman history, was really won by default by Octavian. Technically, Antony and Cleopatra 'won' in the sense that they had broken out of Octavian's blockade, but the campaign was lost. The majority of Antony's ships were taken captive, and gradually his land forces defected to Octavian.

# DEFEAT AND DEATH

The Battle of Actium was a disaster for Antony and Cleopatra and marked the beginning of the end. Although Octavian's blockade was broken by Cleopatra's ships, which – for whatever reason – hoisted sail and left the scene, the battle was lost and Octavian was the victor. A few years later, in commemoration of his victory, Octavian founded the city of Nicopolis ('Victory City', one of several cities of that name in antiquity that were founded to acclaim military victories) on the site where his troops had pitched their camp before the battle, north of the strait leading into the Ambracian Gulf and across from the Actium promontory. The city flourished and was a large and important city in late Roman and Byzantine times, and the modern Greek town Preveza stands immediately south of its extensive ruins.

Octavian also dedicated a monumental campsite memorial, allegedly on the site of his own tent, on a hill north-east of the town. The memorial is mentioned by the historian Cassius Dio (51.1.3), and has recently been excavated. It consists of a podium of masonry fronted by a stepped terrace into which were fixed the bronze rams from the prows of some of Antony's ships. It has been estimated that the monument originally contained rams from about one-tenth of the 350 ships captured. The cuttings in the stone where the rams were placed are well preserved and have provided much information about the types and sizes of the ships deployed in the battle. Furthermore, on the Actian promontory itself, Octavian rebuilt the archaic Temple of Apollo Aktios and enlarged its sanctuary with the embellishment of ship-sheds housing ten of Antony's captured warships. These actions were the perquisites of the victor – the actions of the vanquished were far different.

## Flight

Cleopatra's ships headed south around the coast of the Peloponnese, escaping all pursuers. Antony remained on board her flagship, but Plutarch records that the pair did not meet since Antony spent days alone at the prow holding his head in his hands in despair, either through anger with Cleopatra, or in shame before her. The ship put in at Taenarum, the modern Cape Matapan at the southernmost tip of the middle peninsula stretching south from the Peloponnese. While there, Cleopatra's maidservants allegedly contrived a meeting between Antony and the queen, and persuaded them to dine and sleep together.

They proceeded south to the coast of North Africa. We are told that Antony remained in 'Libya', the general geographical term for the regions west of Egypt, until previously loyal troops there defected to Octavian. Upon learning this, Plutarch says that Antony tried to kill himself, but was prevented from doing so by his friends who sent him onwards to Alexandria. Meanwhile, Cleopatra had continued on to Egypt and Alexandria from Paraetonium, a city in the western desert on the site of the modern town of Mersa Matruh that marked the westernmost boundary of Egypt. Cassius Dio states that Cleopatra hurried to Egypt because of fear that her subjects would revolt if they heard news of the defeat at Actium before her arrival. In order to ensure a welcome for herself, she apparently portrayed her return as a victory, adorning the prows of her ships with garlands and ordering triumphal songs accompanied by flutes. This ploy worked, but two stories of her actions before Antony's arrival indicate her terror and desperate attempts to strengthen her position and arrange an escape route for herself.

Firstly, Cassius Dio records that Cleopatra killed many of the foremost citizens of Alexandria and confiscated their estates, along with many other riches from public and religious sources. According to his account, these men had never been supporters of the queen, and had been gloating over her defeat. The money was to be used to re-equip her army and buy allies. Secondly, Plutarch tells the astonishing story that Cleopatra arranged for her remaining ships to be dragged from the Mediterranean across to the upper part of the Arabian Gulf (presumably roughly along the line of the Suez Canal). She evidently intended to escape with her forces and finances intact to live outside of Egypt, thereby escaping war and seemingly inevitable capture and servitude. We are told that she abandoned this venture when the first ships to cross were burned by the Arabians, and when Antony arrived in Alexandria with the mistaken news that his land forces at Actium were still holding out against Octavian.

## The Next Encounter with Octavian

So, Antony and Cleopatra had retreated back to Egypt. Plutarch states that for a time Antony withdrew from public life, living alone in a seaside residence built on an artificial mole off Pharos Island that was called the Timoneion (after the legendary Athenian misanthrope Timon, the inspiration for Shakespeare's *Timon of Athens*). Possibly he was still afflicted by despair, or he may well have feared an assassination attempt. However, even as the catastrophic news became known of the actual defection of his land forces at Actium and of most other allies, Antony returned to Cleopatra's palace and the two resumed their profligate life of pleasures and luxury. This time, though, there was a difference. 'The Inimitable Livers' society, which had epitomized their extravagant lifestyle at the beginning of their relationship, was dissolved in favour of another association called 'The Partners in Death', formed of those friends who would willingly die together but passed their time in a round of banquets and drinking-bouts as they had done in happier days. We may perhaps see in this an extreme form of escapist behaviour by a couple who realized that the proverbial writing was well and truly upon the wall.

This interpretation is perhaps supported by a colourful anecdote related by Plutarch. He records that at this time Cleopatra amassed a collection of deadly poisons and tested their efficacy upon prisoners condemned to death. (This story is depicted in the painting by Alexandre Cabanel, *Cleopatra Testing Poisons on the Prisoners Condemned to Death* (1887), from which the cover of this book is a detail.) The quickest poisons that Cleopatra tried seemed to produce the most painful deaths, so in her search for a pain-free means of death she turned to experimenting with venomous animals, setting them upon each other. We are told that the bite of an asp produced the easiest death, causing the victims to sink gently into a sleep from which they did not awaken. Plutarch clearly includes this story here to foreshadow Cleopatra's death and the asp's role in it, but if it is true that the queen was testing poisons then it may indicate that even at this stage she saw the inevitability of her own death as she revelled the nights away with Antony.

None the less, Antony and Cleopatra made plans for further warfare against Octavian. Young men were enrolled for military service, including Cleopatra's now teenage son Caesarion and, significantly, Antony's son Antyllus by his former Roman wife Fulvia (the ceremony being the cause of city-wide celebrations for days). Cassius Dio tells us that the enrolment was intended to inspire the Egyptians by the thought that at last they had a man for their king (he does not say which boy he means), and to encourage them to continue the war under the new young leaders in the event of the deaths of Antony and Cleopatra.

Cassius Dio goes on to describe the preparations for war in Egypt, supposedly on land and sea. Antony and Cleopatra tried to summon aid from neighbouring tribes and friendly kings, but also made contingency plans to stir up a revolt in Spain or to change their operations to the Red Sea (perhaps reconsidering Cleopatra's earlier plans to drag her fleet to this area). Dio and Plutarch agree that at this time an embassy was sent to Octavian in Asia Minor, but their accounts of these events and those that follow differ in detail. Dio represents the embassy as an elaborate ruse to divert Octavian's attention from their preparations for war. Peace proposals to Octavian and bribes to his followers were intended to deceive him as to their true intentions and perhaps even to lead to his death by treachery. According to Dio's account, Cleopatra tried to make a deal behind Antony's back. In secret she sent Octavian a golden sceptre, crown, and the royal throne, symbolizing the offer to him of her kingdom. Dio says that she hoped that Octavian might still take pity on her even if he hated Antony. Octavian apparently took the bait. He purportedly made no reply to Antony, but, while publicly threatening Cleopatra to give up her armies and renounce her sovereignty, sent her a secret message that he would pardon her if she killed Antony.

Plutarch recounts that in the embassy to Octavian Cleopatra asked for the kingdom of Egypt for her children, and that Antony requested that he be allowed to live as a private citizen in Athens if he could not do so in Egypt. There is no mention of any secret gift to Cleopatra's enemy here. Again,

Octavian made no answer to Antony, but told Cleopatra, apparently not in secret, that she would receive reasonable treatment if she killed or renounced Antony.

What are we to make of these accounts? Did Octavian really mean his offer, or was he just trying any ploy to rid himself of Antony? Did he really think that Cleopatra had become so frightened by events and disillusioned by Antony that she would even contemplate betraying him to ensure her own survival? Octavian's subsequent actions seem to indicate considerable uncertainty at this point.

Cassius Dio records that Antony and Cleopatra sent a second embassy to Octavian. Cleopatra offered him huge sums of money while Antony tried to win him over by appeals to their kinship and friendship, and surrendered to Octavian a man named Publius Turullius, who was one of the assassins of Julius Caesar. In a telling comment, Dio adds that Antony offered to kill himself if it would ensure Cleopatra's safety. When Octavian killed Turullius but still did not answer, Antony sent to him his son Antyllus with a gift of gold. The gold was kept and the boy returned, but again Octavian did not reply to Antony. He made the

same answer to Cleopatra as before: public threats
and private promises.

Octavian was still unsure how events would
unfold. Dio says that he feared that Antony and
Cleopatra might yet prevail against him, or escape
to Spain or Gaul, or else destroy their vast wealth in
Egypt to prevent him seizing it. Both Dio and
Plutarch attest that Cleopatra had by now collected
together vast royal treasures of precious metals,
gems, and other luxury items and had deposited
them in a magnificent tomb that she was building
for herself in the area of the Palaces, threatening to
burn them all if provoked, and depositing nearby
quantities of flammable materials for this purpose.
To forestall this eventuality, Octavian hatched a
devious scheme of his own. He sent his freedman
Thyrsus to Cleopatra to persuade her that he,
Octavian, was also in love with her. By this act he
appealed to her considerable vanity. Dio says that
'he hoped that by this means at least, since she
thought it her due to be loved by all mankind, she
would make away with Antony and keep herself and
her money unharmed' (51.8.71). Dio adds that 'she
listened to the message by Thyrsus, and believed
that she was really beloved, in the first place

because she wished to be, and in the second place, because she had in the same manner enslaved Caesar's [i.e.Octavian's] father [Julius Caesar] and Antony' (51.9.5). This story is the basis for Dio's presentation of subsequent events as Antony's betrayal by Cleopatra.

Plutarch's version has Thyrsus sent to Alexandria with Octavian's response to the first embassy (he possibly brought the incident forward by misunderstanding the number of embassies). There is no mention of Octavian's supposed confession of love here, but Thyrsus was so conspicuously honoured by the queen, for reasons that are not stated, that Antony became suspicious, flogged him, and sent him away with a message of complaint to Octavian. Plutarch does not say if Antony's suspicions were based on amorous jealousy regarding Thyrsus himself, or political fear. In any event, was Cleopatra's behaviour towards Thyrsus in this version a coded signal to Octavian that she had understood his message (suppressed in Plutarch) and that she was not adverse to considering his offer? And did Antony suspect possible treachery at this stage? However this may be, according to Plutarch Cleopatra backed away and tried to allay

Antony's suspicions with submissive behaviour: she marked her own birthday with little fanfare, for example, but celebrated his with elaborate and costly extravaganzas. Plutarch clearly knows about 'suspicions' of possible betrayal but for him they remain very much in the background.

These divergent views about Cleopatra's intentions are crucial in forming our final assessment of the queen. At this distance it is impossible to say that one ancient account is right and the other wrong. Did Cleopatra deliberately betray her lover to save herself as Dio's sources believe, or did events just go horribly and inexorably wrong, leading to the inevitable rumours of dark betrayal to which even Plutarch's sources allude?

## *Octavian's Invasion of Egypt*

In the summer of 30 BC, the enemies of Antony and Cleopatra attacked Egypt on both sides. Antony first faced the Roman army of Cornelius Gallus, which had occupied Paraetonium in the west. His assaults were unsuccessful on both land and sea. Meanwhile, Octavian returned to Asia Minor after a winter spent in Rome, and, invading Egypt from Syria, captured the city of Pelusium on the easternmost branch of the Nile in its Delta. Dio records that Cleopatra surrendered the city to Octavian in secret because she believed that he was in love with her, and, realizing that the Roman forces could not be withstood, thought that if she yielded now she would be forgiven and retain her kingdom as well as acquiring influence in Rome. Dio furthermore accuses her later of secretly persuading the Alexandrians not to resist Octavian's forces when they arrived there. Plutarch is also aware of the rumour that Pelusium was betrayed, but does not pay it much heed since Cleopatra agreed to the murder of the family of the garrison commander who had surrendered the town.

Antony returned to Alexandria to face in person the advancing army of Octavian. Even Plutarch records that Octavian continued to send Cleopatra messages promising kind treatment so that the queen did not torch the treasures to which he was now drawing near. Antony met the forces of Octavian on the eastern outskirts of Alexandria, routed his cavalry, which was perhaps still tired from marching, and pursued the army as far as its camp. Antony went in triumph to Cleopatra in the palace and presented to her the soldier who had fought most bravely in their defence. The soldier was handsomely rewarded with valuable armour, but later that night defected to Octavian. Plutarch presumably includes this anecdote as a premonition of the disaster to come.

The accounts of the remaining skirmishes are confused. Plutarch alleges that Antony challenged Octavian to individual combat for the second time (the first being before the Battle of Actium). This was refused. Dio says that Antony had tried to turn the loyalties of Octavian's troops by shooting into their camp arrows that held leaflets promising monetary bribes. Octavian, however, intercepted the leaflets and shamed his soldiers into feeling insulted at these aspersions against their loyalty. Their newly inspired zeal in the infantry encounter that followed meant victory for Octavian. According to Dio, Antony next determined to attack by sea but Cleopatra caused the ships to desert. On the other hand, Plutarch at this stage describes a combined land and sea attack. Antony's infantry waited on the hills in front of the city while the fleets drew together. Cleopatra's intervention is not mentioned in his account, but Antony's ships immediately

turned sides, joined Octavian, and sailed together to
attack Alexandria. After this disaster, Antony's
cavalry also deserted to Octavian while his infantry
was defeated in battle. Whatever the truth of the
details of the final encounter, this was the end for
Antony and he withdrew to Alexandria, abandoned
by his forces and utterly defeated.

## The Death of Antony

At the news of the defeat, Cleopatra rushed to her
mausoleum with her servants and locked herself
inside, irrevocably, by lowering a sort of portcullis
of stone secured by bolts and bars. Again, there are
dark hints of treachery. Dio maintains that her
action was a pretence that she feared the approach
of Octavian and preferred suicide, while in reality
she always intended to lure Antony to his death by
her side. We are told that Antony too suspected
betrayal, but that his love for the queen prevented
him from believing it even as he felt enormous pity
for her – more than for himself. In Dio's account
Cleopatra now engineered her ultimate betrayal of
Antony. Taking advantage of his feelings for her, she
hoped that he would kill himself if informed that

she was dead, and, accordingly, she sent him a message to that effect. She was correct, and Antony determined to die. (The false message of her death is also the version used by Shakespeare.)

Plutarch's account is slightly different. After the final battle, he describes Antony as crying out in despair that Cleopatra had betrayed him (although there is no statement elsewhere in Plutarch that she actually had done so). In this version Cleopatra rushed to her tomb and locked herself in out of fear of Antony's rage and madness, and sent a message saying that she was dead, possibly in an attempt to forestall his fury. The effect was the same, but here Antony opined that his grief was because Cleopatra had been the more courageous in taking her life first.

Both sources agree that Antony first begged someone else to kill him. (Plutarch gives this role to a trusty slave named Eros, the Greek word for love.) However, the would-be murderer turned the sword upon himself, whereupon Antony then took courage and stabbed himself. The wound was not immediately fatal, and Antony lay bleeding in agony. Somehow, Cleopatra learned this news, perhaps hearing the outcry outside her tomb. The doors remained closed with the sliding slab of stone, but the upper part of the tomb remained unfinished and provided access. Plutarch says that Cleopatra ordered Antony to be carried to her tomb; Dio says that when bystanders saw the queen peering out and told Antony that she was still alive, he ordered himself to be taken to her.

Antony's death is one of the most dramatic scenes in literature, painting, and film. He was carried to her tomb on a litter. From the upper storey Cleopatra and her two female servants Iras and Charmion lowered ropes, intended for the construction work, and with difficulty drew him up into the tomb. Dio merely says that he died there in Cleopatra's bosom, but Plutarch paints a more colourful scene of the women desperately struggling to lift the weight of the litter even as Antony in mid-air raised his blood-smeared arms towards Cleopatra. He describes a melodramatic deathbed scene inside the tomb, with the queen tearing her garments and beating her breasts in lamentation, while smearing herself with his blood as she calls him her lord and master. After sipping some wine, Antony bade Cleopatra to look after her own safety if she could do so without dishonour, and urged her to put her trust in a man called Proculeius, the most trustworthy of Octavian's companions. However, this would mean that Antony's reported last words are almost certainly fictional, since Proculeius later betrayed the queen through guile. In Plutarch's stirring words, Antony urged her 'not to lament him for his last reverses, but to count him happy for the good things that had been his, since he had become most illustrious of men, had won greatest power, and now had not been ignobly conquered, a Roman by a Roman' (*Life of Antony*, 77 4). And so Marc Antony died.

## Octavian and Cleopatra

Our sources Plutarch and Cassius Dio continue to differ in their accounts of subsequent events. Although the general outline is clear, there are considerable variations in location, chronology, and detail. Plutarch, as befits a biographer who states that he is writing 'lives' not 'histories', presents the more coherent, self-contained narrative, but it is characterized by highly colourful description and dramatic flourishes, especially in the final build-up to Cleopatra's death. We do not know how much of this is a product of Plutarch's imagination. Dio's account is more compressed since it appears in the context of a much longer history, and his treatment, as elsewhere, is more matter-of-fact. In this section I will take into account this variation of the sources only where it is of particular importance or interest.

Octavian was soon informed of Antony's death, either by Cleopatra or by a member of Antony's bodyguard who ran to Octavian with the bloody sword. Cleopatra remained locked in her tomb, and Octavian was determined to get her out alive, both so that she would not burn her treasures in a last act of defiance, and also so that she could adorn his triumphal procession in Rome. Accordingly, Proculeius was sent to the tomb, and conversed with the queen through the locked door at ground level. Cleopatra asked that her children be allowed to have her kingdom, and Proculeius reassured her and told her to trust in Octavian.

According to Plutarch, Cleopatra was captured by deception. The general Gallus was sent to have a second conversation with Cleopatra through the door of the tomb, while Proculeius, by means of a ladder, entered the same upper opening of the tomb where the dying Antony had been taken inside, and descended to the ground floor. When she saw Proculeius behind her, Cleopatra immediately tried to stab herself but was overcome by him and his companion, the freedman Epaphroditus. She was disarmed and searched for any poisons or potential suicide weapon. Epaphroditus was left to guard over her. Plutarch does not mention that she was removed from her tomb, but Dio says that after she had spent several days there embalming Antony's body she was moved to her palace, where she was allowed to keep her retinue (a kindness apparently intended to give her the impression that she would be well treated by Octavian). Plutarch agrees that Octavian gave permission for Cleopatra to bury Antony in a sumptuous and royal fashion, and provided whatever was necessary for this (presumably he was buried in Cleopatra's unfinished mausoleum). The queen fell ill from grief, fever, and pain from the wounds she had inflicted upon herself in lamentation. She welcomed the illness as an excuse to stop eating and thereby end her life. Plutarch says that he used the written account of her physician Olympus for this information. However, she gave up her fast when Octavian threatened the safety of her children, who were now in captivity.

In due course a meeting was arranged between Cleopatra and Octavian, who came to her (possibly in the palace, although this is not certain). This climactic meeting between the two is a favourite theme of western painters (see plate 11) but the ancient sources preserve different accounts. Dio attests that she set the scene carefully, with a splendid apartment and couch prepared and herself adorned in a becoming mourning dress. Her trump card was the memory of Octavian's adopted father, Julius Caesar, whose images and letters she had ready to hand. Dio describes an astonishing scene in which Cleopatra read Caesar's letters to Octavian, kissed them and prostrated herself before Caesar's images, bewailing her fate prettily and using every emotional ploy she could think of. We are told that Octavian was quite moved by the queen and her performance, but pretended to be unaffected. When he neither looked at her, nor said anything about her kingdom, nor mentioned anything about the love he was supposed to feel for her, Cleopatra changed her strategy. She threw himself at his feet and implored him to allow her to die so that she could be reunited with Antony. Octavian was not moved to pity by these entreaties, and did not answer her.

Dio implies that the interview ended there. Octavian feared that her suicide would deprive him of her appearance in his triumph, so he urged her to be of good cheer and took kindly care of her so that she would not kill herself. Cleopatra saw through his ploy and was desperate to avoid such a public humiliation in Rome. She persisted in her pleas to him to allow her to die in any manner, but Octavian was resolute. Reverting again to guile, Cleopatra pretended to change her mind and to trust Octavian and his wife Livia. She said she would sail to Rome of her own accord and packed various gifts from her treasures to distribute when she arrived. By feigning cooperation she hoped that the suicide watch over her would be relaxed. So it was, and in this way Cleopatra created the circumstances for her death.

Plutarch's account of the fateful meeting describes an ill, dishevelled, and pitiful Cleopatra awaiting Octavian, clad only in a tunic and lying on a pallet, although he says that her charm and beauty were not totally extinguished. In this account she immediately threw herself at his feet, but was helped back on to her bed. A conversation ensued in which the queen tried to justify her actions to

Octavian (one reason being her purported previous fear of Antony), but she was refuted on every point. Here, too, Cleopatra was forced to change her tactics and she tried to arouse Octavian's pity as one who desired to live even in defeat. Again her treasures came into play: she allegedly gave Octavian a list of them all but was denounced by a servant, who said that that she had kept some behind. Turning misfortune to advantage, Cleopatra persuaded Octavian that the reserved articles were intended as gifts for his sister and wife, whose intercession on her behalf might make him more merciful towards herself. Octavian went off convinced that she intended to live, and promised splendid treatment at his hands. As Plutarch states, Octavian thought that he had deceived Cleopatra, but she had in reality deceived him. The stage was set.

## The Death of Cleopatra

It will not by now come as a surprise to learn that the death of Cleopatra is shrouded in mystery and uncertainty. Before the final act, Plutarch inserts the story of her visit to Antony's tomb. According to Plutarch, Cleopatra had been warned by a

companion of Octavian, a man named Dolabella
who had fallen under her spell, that she and her
children were to be sent to Rome in three days.
Cleopatra begged Octavian to be allowed to pour
libations at Antony's tomb. Permission was granted,
and the queen was carried there in the company of
her attendants. Plutarch recounts an impassioned
speech as Cleopatra embraced the coffin. She
bewailed her fate as a captive, voiced her fear of
dying in Italy, and implored him and his Roman
gods to spare her the humiliation of a triumph and
to allow her to be buried in Egypt with him. Such
stock sentiments are probably dramatic inventions
by Plutarch, since no other source mentions a visit
to Antony's tomb, but if the incident (if not the
exact words) had indeed occurred it supports Dio's
remark that Cleopatra had been moved earlier from
the tomb to the palace – hence her return now to
the tomb.

Plutarch then records that Cleopatra bathed,
adorned herself in fine apparel, and dined lavishly
(presumably back at the palace since various people
enter and depart). During dinner a servant brought
in a basket of large, beautiful figs for the queen.
Because he had freely offered some to the guards,

they assumed the figs were not dangerous and allowed him to pass. A sealed message was then given to Epaphroditus to take to Octavian. He was told that the message concerned another matter, but in reality it contained Cleopatra's final pleas to be buried next to Antony. The queen sent away everyone but her two maidservants Iras and Charmion, and closed the doors. Upon opening the message, Octavian instantly realized what was afoot and sent messengers at the run to intervene. The guards had been aware of nothing, but when the doors were opened Cleopatra was found in her royal regalia lying dead on her couch. Iras was dying at her feet, and Charmion expired while trying to arrange the diadem on the queen's head (see plate 12 for an imaginative depiction of the deathbed scene).

Dio states that Octavian was astonished at the news of her death, and even sent Psylli (Libyans renowned for curing snakebite by sucking out the venom) in an effort to revive her. But Cleopatra was gone, on 10 August 30 BC, at the age of thirty-nine. Octavian was allegedly moved by admiration and pity at her death, though aggrieved that he had been deprived of the full glory of his victory since Cleopatra could now not be taken as his prisoner to Rome.

He none the less ordered a splendid and royal burial for Queen Cleopatra VII next to the body of Antony, presumably in the mausoleum, and a fitting funeral for her servants.

At the time of writing, it is impossible to say if the Tomb of Cleopatra will ever be found. It looked highly unlikely in the years before the new excavations around the harbour of Alexandria, but archaeology holds many surprises and the ancient city may yet yield its treasures. Speculation as to the precise manner of Cleopatra's death is irrepressible but futile. Popular imagination from Shakespeare to Hollywood has seized upon the notion of the asp in the basket of figs, and Octavian himself (who was much closer to events than almost anyone else) seems to have subscribed to this notion since Plutarch states that an image of the queen with an asp attached to her was carried in his triumphal procession when it was finally celebrated in 29 BC.

But our ancient sources are uncertain. Both Dio and Plutarch say that no one knew for sure how she died. Plutarch knew about the asp in the figs, and another version of the creature being kept in a water jar, biting her when disturbed. No viper was found in the chamber, though some alleged that the trail of a serpent had been seen on the seafront, near the windows of her chamber. Cleopatra was also said to have kept poison in a hollow comb in her hair. There was no evidence of the effects of poison on her body, but some attested to two small pricks on her arm. Dio knew the same stories, so presumably he and Plutarch here used the same source, except Dio's version has an asp hidden in flowers rather than figs. He also mentions that others declared that she had a hairpin smeared with poison in her hair, which she pricked into her arm thus causing the visible mark.

But the queen and her two servants died at about the same time. Perhaps the story of the snake or snakes was a colourful invention. Unless there were several poisonous serpents available, the trio must have had access to artificial poisons as well to achieve the death of them all. Earlier Roman sources such as the first-century BC poets Virgil, Horace, and Propertius do mention two snakes, the last in the context of the image of Cleopatra in Octavian's procession. The double cobra was indeed the symbol of the Egyptian royal house, so that two serpents might be thought to be appropriate means of suicide, but we still need a method of death for the third woman, since snakes take time to replenish their venom after a bite.

The ancient sources agree that it was suicide but differ as to the method. Certain modern scholars have suggested that the scene was a cover-up for Octavian's murder of Cleopatra, or, at least, for his acquiescence to her death. But he had no reason to want her dead in this way, and not even Octavian's bitterest enemies in antiquity suggested his connivance as, in my opinion, they surely would have done if it were even suspected, since the Emperor Augustus (as Octavian became) had a very hostile press. The final word, therefore, belongs to the poet Horace, who was quoted in the Introduction (see pp. 3–4):

> She even dared to gaze with face serene upon her fallen palace; courageous, too, to handle poisonous asps, that she might draw black venom to her heart, waxing bolder as she resolved to die; scorning, in sooth, the thought of being borne, a queen no longer, on hostile galleys to grace a glorious triumph – no craven woman she! (*Odes*, 1.37.25–32)

# SEVEN

# HISTORICAL REFLECTIONS

The death of Cleopatra VII signalled the end of the Ptolemaic Empire of Egypt. Caesarion, her alleged son by Caesar, was executed on Octavian's orders in 30 BC while fleeing towards India via Ethiopia. Her three children by Antony suffered the humilation of marching in Octavian's Roman triumph in 29 BC, but their lives had been spared, at least for a time. They were brought up in Rome in the house of Antony's divorced wife Octavia, who after his death magnanimously raised his children, their mutual children, and her own children under the same roof. The fates of the boys Alexander Helios and Ptolemy Philadelphus are unknown (though the fact that we hear nothing about them afterwards suggests that they were soon killed), but the daughter Cleopatra Selene later married King Juba II of Mauretania in North Africa, a client-king supported on his throne by Rome. Cleopatra VII's line lived on for a time in her grandson from this union, Ptolemy of Mauretania, who inherited the throne but was executed in AD 40 by the Roman Emperor Caligula. Thus the Ptolemaic lineage was extinguished, in so far as we can trace it.

The Hellenistic Age is traditionally reckoned to span the years from the death of Alexander the Great in 323 BC to that of Cleopatra VII in 30 BC, this 'end' marking the capitulation of the last Hellenistic Empire to Rome. Of course, such arbitrary divisions of historical periods were unknown at the time, and life went on, although it was different. The later history of Roman Egypt does not concern us here, except to reiterate that Egypt became a province of the Roman Empire under Octavian, and it remained the personal property of the Roman Emperor of the day. Alexandria grew to become the second largest city of the empire, and the prosperity of Egypt was exploited throughout the following centuries. Alexandria remained a great trading entrepôt between east and west, and grain exported from the fertile Nile Valley was essential in feeding the growing urban classes of Rome. Alexandria continued to flourish as a great Graeco-Roman city and centre of Greek culture until it was captured by the Arabs in AD 642. The current archaeological excavations in the eastern harbour may shed light on just how great a city it was.

It is difficult to draw any conclusions as such about the fall of the Ptolemaic Empire and the death of Cleopatra. The glittering culture and sophistication of the court life of Hellenistic Alexandria, and the impressive urban design of the city, have been described in Chapter Two. The turbulent political history and the chaotic dynastic upheavals aside, Ptolemaic Alexandria's role in the history of Greek literature and in the growth of learning in many different spheres proclaims its supreme place in one of the most important eras of ancient Greek history. From the viewpoint of the Greek East, the Roman conquest of Ptolemaic Egypt – the last of the Hellenistic powers to fall under her sway – was a calamity of immense proportions. From then on, it was a different world, one in which Rome was unquestionably dominant. With the benefit of hindsight and from our knowledge of the subsequent history of the Roman Empire, we may be forgiven for seeing Rome's eventual domination of the Mediterranean as inevitable, as did many contemporary historians. In this book, however, we are dealing with the human tragedy of a young woman who lost her throne, her country, her lovers, and her life through the misfortune of living in a time of inexorable historical change.

## The Appearance of Cleopatra

Cleopatra's physical appearance has been a source of speculation throughout the ages. Popular imagination has glorified her as a *femme fatale* whose legendary beauty enslaved the likes of Caesar and Antony and resulted in tragic historical consequences. A useful comparison with this picture of Cleopatra might be the fabled Helen of Troy and the disaster she brought in her wake. Current culture has fuelled this assumption through the choice of the most glamorous and beautiful women of their time to play Cleopatra on stage and screen. However, there is a little contemporary evidence about Cleopatra's appearance, and it must be from this that any discussion stems.

The Hellenistic rulers issued coins with dynastic portrait heads on the obverse, and various symbolic images on the reverse. This iconography seems obvious to modern readers whose states also issue coinage with the portrait of the head of state or venerable figures from the historical past on the obverse, along with powerful national symbols on the reverse, but this practice in Greek antiquity dated only from the time of Alexander the Great in the fourth century BC. These issues of 'portrait-coins' and, indeed, the development of ancient portraiture in general – both broad and fascinating topics – are not our business here, but it is generally held that Hellenistic portrait-coins have a basically lifelike if idealized resemblance to their subjects. They were not intended to reflect the true personality of the ruler, but rather the ways in which the ruler preferred to be presented to his subjects. Since ancient coins were minted with the name of the ruler in whose reign they were minted, well-preserved Hellenistic coins can be dated exactly to the regnal years of the monarch in question (when known). These royal images give us some clues about the actual appearance of those upon whom they were modelled, but cannot, of course, be considered anything approaching a true-to-life portrait or modern photograph.

Cleopatra VII was the only Ptolemaic queen to mint coins in her own right. Fortunately, coins of Cleopatra are known, which enable us to form some assessment of her appearance and are the basis upon which any other alleged likeness of her in other artistic media must be measured. There are two main coin types of Cleopatra, conventionally known as the 'Alexandrian' or 'Hellenistic' portrait type, and the very different 'Romanized' type (see plates 8 and 9).* The so-called 'Alexandrian' type depicts Cleopatra as a typical Ptolemaic, Macedonian queen. It is not a particularly flattering portrait, but shows a woman in early middle age with strong features, a conventional 'melon' hairstyle with a bun at the back, and a royal diadem. A variant of this type depicts Cleopatra holding her infant son Caesarion, with the royal sceptre in the background. These coins, minted in Egypt, appear throughout her reign, and it has been argued that

---

\* For a discussion of these coin types, see Smith, *Hellenistic Sculpture*, p. 209.

they were designed for use within her kingdom. The 'Romanized' type presents Cleopatra as the consort of her patron Marc Antony, whose head appears on the reverse side of the coins. This portrait is less flattering, depicting Cleopatra as older and with a long neck (possibly with a goitre?) and a prominent hooked nose. These coins were minted outside Egypt and were presumably intended for foreign usage in lands under Roman control. Professor R.R.R. Smith (in *Hellenistic Sculpture*) contends that the different likenesses were designed to reflect Cleopatra's dual roles as Ptolemaic queen in her own country and as a client-queen of Rome.

The 'Alexandrian' coin type has been used to identify two marble portrait heads as likenesses of Cleopatra: the Vatican Cleopatra and the Berlin Cleopatra (see plate 1), although there is disagreement as to whether the latter head is ancient or modern. The heads are remarkably similar, and are probably copies of the same Alexandrian portrait of the queen (Plutarch in his *Life of Antony* (86.5) refers to statues of Cleopatra erected in Alexandria which were not torn down after her death). The heads depict a full-faced mature woman with hair drawn back into a bun and bound with the royal diadem.

The features are pleasant but the face is not conventionally beautiful by modern standards. From this slim evidence of coins and sculpture it seems that Plutarch's observations about her appearance are substantially correct: 'For her beauty, as we are told, was in itself not altogether incomparable, nor such as to strike those who saw her . . .' (*Life of Antony*, 27.2). (Dio, however, claims that she was of 'unsurpassing beauty' (42.34.4).)

There is a view held in some quarters, especially in America, that Cleopatra was a Negro, therefore 'black' in the modern usage of the term. This view arises out of the highly controversial book by Martin Bernal, *Black Athena. The Afroasiatic Roots of Classical Civilization*, in which he argues forcefully for an Afrocentric origin for much of ancient Mediterranean culture. This book has stimulated a vigorous scholarly debate, and its ramifications are still being discussed some ten years after publication. Starting from the assumption that all Egyptians were black (itself an incorrect premise), it has subsequently been argued by others that Cleopatra was an 'empowered' black African queen, and, as such, she has become in some quarters an icon of the black feminist movement. Bernal's main thesis is far beyond the scope of this book, and it has been debated by scholars more qualified than I.* I certainly do not wish to attempt to dethrone role models for those who find them inspiring, but it *is* within the scope of this volume to discuss Cleopatra's appearance.

The above theory of Cleopatra's skin colour flies in the face of the fact that the Ptolemaic dynasty were in origin Macedonians from northern Greece. It has been outlined above that most Ptolemaic kings made incestuous marriages with their female relatives, or married princesses from other Graeco-Macedonian dynasties. There is no evidence of illegitimate royal liaisons with women not related to the Ptolemies that produced rivals to the throne, or of heirs to the throne who were not the sons of royal mothers, at least in the early generations of the dynasty. The Ptolemaic bloodline, so far as it can be traced, seems to have remained European in the

* For the most level-headed discussions of Bernal's theories, see Lefkowitz and Rogers (eds), *Black Athena Revisited*, especially the article by Frank M. Snowden, Jr, 'Bernal's "Blacks" and the Afrocentrists', pp. 112–28, on the general question of colour in Greek antiquity, and on the colour of Cleopatra in particular.

third and second centuries BC. It is well known, however, that Cleopatra's father Ptolemy XII Auletes *was* illegitimate. *If* the mother of Auletes had been a Nubian concubine (for example) of his father Ptolemy IX, there may have been African blood in Cleopatra, but the fact remains that there is absolutely no evidence about the identity of the mother of Auletes. This woman may have been black, but, equally, she may not have been.

The question of Cleopatra's mother has also been discussed at length in Chapter Three. Certainty is impossible, but the suggestion that she was the daughter of Auletes's sister-wife Cleopatra V Tryphaena cannot in the end be refuted. If so, Cleopatra V would have been the same colour as her husband (assuming that they were full brother and sister), but still there is no evidence for the identity of their mother. If Cleopatra VII really *was* the daughter of a second wife of Auletes, as some have thought, there is absolutely no clue as to the identity of this woman or her racial background, so it is impossible to say anything useful. Again, we just do not know what colour Cleopatra was. This is not my distortion of the evidence in order to argue a politically incorrect line; there simply is no evidence.

Two other points are relevant. Others have pointed out that hostile Roman writers who were eager to paint Cleopatra in an unfavourable light might well have emphasized a black colour to make her more foreign to Roman eyes. But they are silent on this issue, which may argue that her colour was not something that was regarded as unusual. A stronger argument is that there are no identifiably negroid features in any of the known portraits of Cleopatra, at a time when Greek artists had accurately been depicting negroes for centuries.

## Cleopatra the Woman

In light of the above inadequate evidence for Cleopatra's physical appearance, unanswerable questions remain: What was Cleopatra really like? What was her evident attraction for men? Was she a slave to love or a calculating politician? Plutarch goes on, in the passage quoted above (p. 99), to testify to the charm of her personality and conversation:

. . . converse with her had an irrestible charm, and her presence, combined with the persuasiveness of her discourse and the character which was somehow diffused about her behaviour towards others, had something stimulating about it. There was sweetness also in the tones of her voice . . .' (*Life of Antony*, 27.2–3)

None the less, it will be clear from the preceding chapters that there is not enough evidence in the ancient sources to answer the above questions satisfactorily. This essentially 'blank canvas' has given writers, painters, and film directors free rein to paint their own interpretations of her, and Cleopatra's fame has ensured her unremitting popularity as a subject. Wildly differing interpretations have resulted (see, for example, plate 5, a highly romantic fantasy of Cleopatra's arrival in her barge by the British painter William Etty, and plate 6, Lawrence Alma-Tadema's brooding depiction of Antony visiting Cleopatra who awaits him on her barge). The following discussion is by necessity based upon extrapolation from the few facts we know.

## The Egyptian Cleopatra

Although in the western world many portraits and films have depicted Cleopatra in Egyptian guise, it must not be forgotten that the Ptolemaic dynasty was Greek in origin. Certainly the Ptolemaic kings and queens were represented as Egyptian pharaohs in traditional dress, poses, and activities for the benefit of the Egyptian population. There exist various free-standing statues of decidedly Egyptian-looking Ptolemies, and also sculpted frieze reliefs in similar style in native temples constructed during the Ptolemaic period, such as Denderah, Edfu, and Kom Ombo (see plate 9 for an Egyptianizing depiction of Cleopatra and her son Caesarion as Isis and Horus from the Temple of Hathor at Denderah). From the time of Ptolemy V, the king was actually crowned as pharaoh in a ritualized coronation ceremony dating back centuries. One may interpret this Egyptianizing iconography as the calculated attempt on the part of the Ptolemies to present themselves to the native population as traditional rulers who could claim political legitimacy in Egypt. Their private views on the matter are unknown, if indeed they had strong ones, but clearly their main political orientation was towards the other Hellenistic powers of the day.

However Greek the culture of Alexandria, it appears that various Egyptian artistic elements were adopted and blended with Greek motifs to create a distinctive hybrid Graeco-Egyptian artistic style, which appears to have become more prevalent over time. Some Greek writers of the early Hellenistic period describe characteristic Egyptian artistic elements with a sense of curiosity, and Alexandrian necropolis areas in particular reveal a proliferation of Egyptian architectural and artistic motifs. The new finds of sphinxes and Egyptianizing statues from the eastern harbour at Alexandria may show that this artistic syncretism was more common at an early date than was previously thought.

The above serves as a prelude to the question of how 'Egyptian' Cleopatra was, presiding as she did over a court that we may suppose to be primarily Greek in language and custom. The Eyptianizing portraits of her, given their context within the whole tradition of Ptolemaic native iconography, cannot be used to judge this issue. Presumably Cleopatra was a native Greek speaker, and spoke Greek or Latin to both Caesar and Antony, whether directly or through interpreters (we are told that she rarely needed interpreters with 'Barbarians', but we do not know if she spoke Latin or the Romans Greek). Plutarch states that she was the first

Ptolemaic ruler to speak Egyptian in addition to many other near-eastern languages, which may or may not indicate a definite policy on her part. Perhaps it was a calculated political gesture, or perhaps she had picked up the demotic Egyptian language as a child from the palace servants, or had even studied it, and was overheard to use it in public by someone who thought it remarkable enough to note. More telling is the fact that she used the epithet 'Philopatris' ('Fatherland-loving') as one of her royal titles, and she is attested to have paid particular homage to Egyptian cults. If her palace is discovered in the eastern harbour at Alexandria, we may gain clearer insights into these questions.

It has been seen above that Cleopatra symbolized 'eastern' decadence as far as the Roman world was concerned: an 'eastern' queen whose sumptuous court life had lured two aristocratic Romans away from staunch Roman virtues. But I would argue that 'eastern' in this context does not mean 'Egyptian' in the precise definition of the term, but refers rather to the royal lifestyle with its trappings of extreme wealth and conspicuous display that characterized those eastern Hellenistic monarchies, and which was in sharp contrast to what the Romans liked to think were the virtues of the Roman Republic. For the previous two centuries Roman generals on campaign in the Greek East had encountered the splendour of the Hellenistic courts, and were as attracted to the perquisites of this lifestyle as they may have been secretly shocked by its luxury and pomp. Several of these generals appear to have affected the style of the Hellenistic monarchs (this is seen, for example, in the lavish nature of their triumphs in Rome, the issue of coinage with their portraits on the obverse, and in self-glorifying monuments). However, until the advent of Cleopatra, Roman nobles had not become ensnared into personal relationships and long-term romantic/political liaisons with non-Roman, eastern monarchs. Given the threatening political climate in Rome at the time, it is not surprising that the Romans were alarmed, and hence outraged, by Cleopatra's perceived influence.

## Epilogue

And what of Cleopatra's personal allure? It appears from her extant portraits (see above) that she was not a conventional beauty, yet she had love affairs

and children with two of the most powerful
Romans of their day. She was twenty-odd when she
met Caesar, and twenty-eight when she met Antony.
This is hardly old by modern standards, but she
would have been considered a mature woman in
antiquity. It is doubtful that the arranged dynastic
marriages to her two younger brothers (both then
mere boys) were anything other than officially
convenient. Did they bring her any personal
happiness, or just fleeting political stability? The
revolt against Cleopatra by Ptolemy XIII and his
courtiers, and the murder of the second brother,
Ptolemy XIV on her orders, point decidedly in the
latter direction. What then can we make of the
legendary romances with Caesar and Antony?
Plutarch says that her attraction lay in her skills at
conversation rather than in her appearance. Perhaps
this, and the undoubted attractions of the luxurious
Alexandrian court, were enough for army men far
from home and in powerful positions. Were these
relationships more than opportunism on one or
both sides? Was Cleopatra the manipulator, or was
she the victim?

This question, infuriatingly, does not have a
clear answer. Cleopatra was a young queen on an

unsteady throne. Egypt could not help but be drawn into the wider Mediterranean picture given Rome's increasing dominance in the region, but the chaos of the Roman civil wars between rival protagonists struggling for power meant that the final outcome was highly uncertain. Cleopatra must have foreseen that she needed a strong protector to secure her throne once the Egyptian nationalists, joined by her brother and husband Ptolemy XIII, rose against her. At this time Caesar, now the clear winner over his rival Pompey (who was murdered as he arrived in Egypt), would have seemed a safe bet. Cleopatra judged this correctly, since Caesar's troops fought the Alexandrian War on her behalf against her brother, and restored her to her throne.

Despite the anecdotal evidence of the ancient sources, it is impossible to say whether or not Cleopatra viewed their affair initially as more than a fair recompense for favours granted. Caesar's feelings are unknown. He was at the time married to his fourth wife, the well-connected Roman Calpurnia, and was fifty-two years old to Cleopatra's twenty-one. Was this more to him than a pleasant dalliance that opportunity placed in his

path? Presumably Caesar and Cleopatra's Nile
cruise was enjoyable enough, but the birth of
Caesarion in the next year put things on a different
footing. The political ramifications of the birth of a
child who had equal claim both to the Egyptian
throne and to Roman power must have been as
welcome to Cleopatra as they were inconvenient to
Caesar. Her evident desperation now to attach
herself to Caesar's star is clear from her astonishing
decision to move herself and her child to Rome,
but why did she do this? Was she deeply in love?
Was she afraid that her position in Egypt was still
untenable? Did she really hope that Caesar would
divorce Calpurnia, marry her, and ensure the
legitimacy of their son? However this may be, their
sojourn in Rome, the home of Calpurnia, from
46–44 BC was an embarrassment to Caesar on his
home ground, and Cleopatra's absence from Egypt
can hardly have helped her cause in that kingdom.

Caesar's assassination in 44 BC changed the
picture utterly. Cleopatra was thrown back on to
her own resources, returned to Egypt, and
strengthened her power within the country by
ordering the murder of her second brother and then
husband Ptolemy XIV. In Rome, the rivalry over

Caesar's political heritage was intense, but it gradually polarized between Antony and Caesar's adopted son Octavian. Since Antony's power base was in the east, it was perhaps inevitable that he should meet the one remaining Hellenistic monarch there, although his alleged summons was to make Cleopatra answer charges of aiding Antony's former rival Cassius. Plutarch presents their relationship as a great love affair, with Antony dazzled both by the queen and by the splendour of her entertainments. Perhaps this is true. The association did last for eleven years, but, however passionate their relationship may have been, politics swiftly intervened. The growing power of Octavian and the increasing Roman hostility towards Antony meant that Antony and Cleopatra's strongest position lay in establishing a joint rule together and with their children in the east.

The above analysis suggests that Cleopatra was a realist who took advantage of various, albeit unorthodox, routes to ensure her own salvation. Her political cunning and capacity for survival meant that her country remained independent from direct Roman rule for longer than the odds might have suggested, and a marriage alliance with a

Roman ruler might have ensured Egypt's future security as well as her own position on the throne. To this extent, she appears to have been ruled by her head.

Yet one cannot but hope that Cleopatra, who saw her world crumble around her, her lovers die, and doubtless foresaw towards the end that the days of an independent Egypt were numbered, experienced some transient happiness in her life with Caesar and Antony, even if it was not the rosy picture dreamt up by Hollywood. Was she perhaps partly ruled by her heart? On the one hand, once Antony had gone and Octavian drew near, there was no foreseeable political or personal future left to her. Her suicide meant that Octavian was robbed of his ultimate victory over her, and she was spared the humiliating public consequences of defeat. Do we therefore praise her for remaining in control and being the arbiter of her own fate? Or, on the other hand, did she kill herself for lost love and a broken heart, even though her young children would be left alone and highly vulnerable, and her country leaderless, at a critical time? Was she, on this reckoning, ultimately a self-centred, emotional woman who took the coward's way out, afraid to face the inevitable and abandoning those to whom she had responsibilities?

Ultimately, in terms of her private life and in the circumstances of her death, the real Cleopatra eludes us to the end.

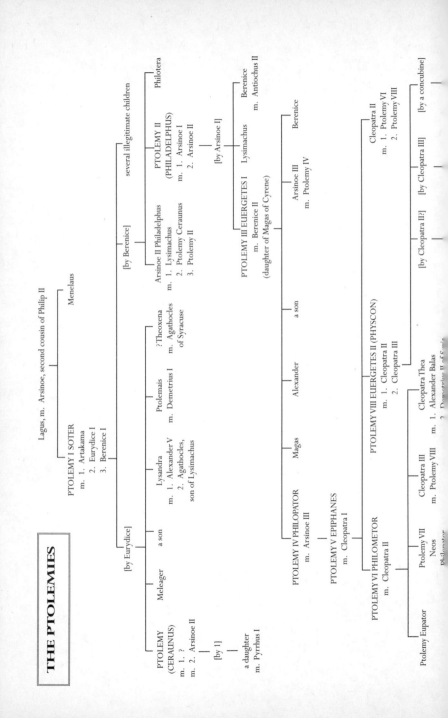

THE PTOLEMIES

Lagus, m. Arsinoe, second cousin of Philip II

Menelaus

PTOLEMY I SOTER
m. 1. Artakama
   2. Eurydice I
   3. Berenice I

[by Eurydice]

[by Berenice]                                    several illegitimate children

Meleager    a son                    Lysandra          Ptolemais       ?Theoxena        Arsinoe II Philadelphus      PTOLEMY II          Philotera
                                     m. 1. Alexander V  m. Demetrius I  m. Agathocles    m. 1. Lysimachus           (PHILADELPHUS)
                                        2. Agathocles,                  of Syracuse         2. Ptolemy Ceraunus    m. 1. Arsinoe I
                                        son of Lysimachus                                   3. Ptolemy II             2. Arsinoe II

PTOLEMY                                                                                                              [by Arsinoe I]
(CERAUNUS)
m. 1. ?                                                                                                             Lysimachus    Berenice
   2. Arsinoe II                                                                                                                  m. Antiochus II

[by 1]                                                                               PTOLEMY III EUERGETES I
                                                                                     m. Berenice II
a daughter                                                          Berenice         (daughter of Magas of Cyrene)
m. Pyrrhus I                                                                                           Arsinoe III
                                                                                                       m. Ptolemy IV

                                      Magas        Alexander        a son

PTOLEMY IV PHILOPATOR
m. Arsinoe III                                                                       PTOLEMY VIII EUERGETES II (PHYSCON)
                                                                                     m. 1. Cleopatra II                Cleopatra II
PTOLEMY V EPIPHANES                                                                     2. Cleopatra III              m. 1. Ptolemy VI
m. Cleopatra I                                                                                                           2. Ptolemy VIII

PTOLEMY VI PHILOMETOR                                            Cleopatra III      Cleopatra Thea
m. Cleopatra II                                                 m. Ptolemy VIII     m. 1. Alexander Balas
                                                                                       2. Demetrius II of Syria
Ptolemy Eupator    Ptolemy VII                                  [by Cleopatra II?]  [by Cleopatra II]   [by Cleopatra III]   [by a concubine]
                   Neos
                   Philometor

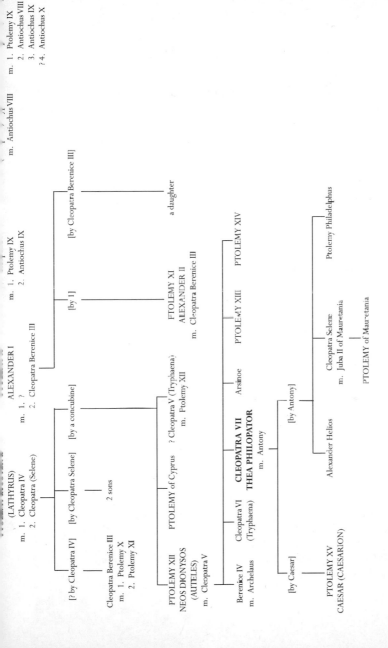

From *The Cambridge Ancient History*, volume IX (The Last Age of the Roman Republic 146–43 BC), eds J.A. Cook, A.W. Lintott, and E. Rawson (Cambridge University Press, 1994), pp. 778–9.

# BIBLIOGRAPHY

Appian. *Civil Wars*, vols III and IV of Appian's *Roman History*, trs. Horace White, 4 vols, Loeb Classical Library, London, William Heinemann Ltd, and Cambridge, Mass., Harvard University Press, 1912–13

Bernal, Martin. *Black Athena. The Afroasiatic Roots of Classical Civilization*, London, Free Association Books, 1987

Bowman, A.K. *Egypt after the Pharaohs, 332 BC–AD 642*, Berkeley, Los Angeles, and London, The University of California Press, 1986

Bowman, A.K., Champlin, E., and Lintott, A. (eds). *The Cambridge Ancient History*, vol. X (The Augustan Empire, 43 BC–AD 69), 2nd edn, Cambridge, Cambridge University Press, 1996, chapter 1

Bradford, E.D.S. *Cleopatra*, London, Hodder and Stoughton Ltd, 1971

Caesar, Julius. *Alexandrian War*, in *Alexandrian, African and Spanish Wars*, trs. A.G. Way, Loeb Classical Library, London, William Heinemann Ltd, and Cambridge Mass., Harvard University Press, 1955

——. *Civil War*, trs. A.G. Peskett, Loeb Classical Library, London, William Heinemann Ltd, and Cambridge, Mass., Harvard University Press, 1914

Carter, J.M. *The Battle of Actium. The Rise and Triumph of Augustus Caesar*, London, Hamish Hamilton, 1970

*Dio's Roman History*, trs E. Cary, 9 vols, Loeb Classical Library, London, William Heinemann Ltd, and Cambridge, Mass., Harvard University Press, 1914–27

Empereur, Jean-Yves. *Alexandria Rediscovered*, London, British Museum Press, 1998

# Bibliography

Flamarion, Edith. *Cleopatra: from History to Legend*, London, Thames and Hudson, 1997

Foss, Michael. *The Search for Cleopatra*, London, Michael O'Mara Books Ltd (in association with BBC *TimeWatch*), 1997

Grant, Michael. *Cleopatra*, London, Weidenfeld & Nicolson, 1972

Herodotus. *Histories*, trs. A.D. Godley, 4 vols, Loeb Classical Library, London, William Heinemann Ltd, and Cambridge, Mass., Harvard University Press, 1920–5

Horace. *The Odes and Epodes*, trs. C.E. Bennett, Loeb Classical Library, London, William Heinemann Ltd, and Cambridge, Mass., Harvard University Press, rev. edn 1927

Hughes-Hallett, Lucy. *Cleopatra: Histories, Dreams and Distortions*, London, Bloomsbury Publishing Ltd, 1990

Lefkowitz, M. and Rogers, G.M. (eds). *Black Athena Revisited*, Chapel Hill, North Carolina University Press, 1996

Plutarch. *Life of Antony*, vol. 9 of Plutarch's *Lives*, trs. B. Perrin, Loeb Classical Library, London, William Heinemann Ltd, and Cambridge, Mass., Harvard University Press, 1920. For the *Life of Antony*, see the excellent commentary by C.B.R. Pelling, *Plutarch: Life of Antony*, Cambridge, Cambridge University Press, 1988

——. *Life of Caesar*, vol. 7 of Plutarch's *Lives*, trs. B. Perrin, Loeb Classical Library, London, William Heinemann Ltd, and Cambridge, Mass., Harvard University Press, 1919

Samson, Julia. *Nefertiti and Cleopatra: Queen-Monarchs of Ancient Egypt*, 2nd edn, London, The Rubicon Press, 1990

Shakespeare, William. *Antony and Cleopatra* (1607/8)

Shaw, George Bernard, *Caesar and Cleopatra* (1899)

Smith, R.R.R. *Hellenistic Sculpture. A Handbook*, London, Thames and Hudson, 1991

Suetonius, *Life of the Deified Julius*, vol. I of Suetonius, *Lives of the Caesars*, trs. John C. Rolfe, 2 vols, Loeb Classical Library, London, William Heinemann Ltd, and Cambridge, Mass., Harvard University Press, rev. edn 1997–8

Tarn, W.W. and Charlesworth, M.P. *Octavian, Antony, and Cleopatra*, Cambridge, Cambridge University Press, 1965

Volkmann, Hans. *Cleopatra: A Study in Politics and Propaganda*, tr. T.J. Cadoux, London, Elek Books Ltd, 1958

# POCKET BIOGRAPHIES

*Beethoven*
Anne Pimlott Baker

*Mao Zedong*
Delia Davin

*Scott of the Antarctic*
Michael De-la-Noy

*Alexander the Great*
E.E. Rice

*Sigmund Freud*
Stephen Wilson

*Marilyn Monroe*
Sheridan Morley and
Ruth Leon

*Rasputin*
Harold Shukman

*Jane Austen*
Helen Lefroy

*Ellen Terry*
Moira Shearer

*David Livingstone*
C.S. Nicholls

*Abraham Lincoln*
H.G. Pitt

*Marie and Pierre
Curie*
John Senior

*Margot Fonteyn*
Alastair Macaulay

*Enid Blyton*
George Greenfield

*Winston Churchill*
Robert Blake

*George IV*
Michael De-la-Noy

*Christopher Wren*
James Chambers

*Che Guevara*
Andrew Sinclair

*W.G. Grace*
Donald Trelford

*The Brontës*
Kathryn White

*Lawrence of Arabia*
Jeremy Wilson

*Christopher Columbus*
Peter Riviere

*Martin Luther King*
Harry Harmer

*Genghis Khan*
James Chambers

*James Dean*
William Hall

*Cleopatra*
E.E. Rice

*John Ruskin*
Francis O'Gorman

For a copy of our complete list or details of other Sutton titles, please contact Emma Leitch at Sutton Publishing Limited, Phoenix Mill, Thrupp, Stroud, Gloucestershire, GL5 2BU